MICHAEL

JEWISH LAW AND THE
American Thanksgiving Celebration

SECULAR OR RELIGIOUS HOLIDAY?

Including unpublished teshuvot by
Rabbi David Cohen, Rabbi Feivel Cohen,
and **Rabbi Ephraim Greenblatt**,
as well as teshuvot from other leading poskim
with appendices on other American holidays
and an examination of the kashrut of turkey.

The Institute for
Jewish Research and Publications

Cambridge, MA • 2024

Jewish Law and the American Thanksgiving Celebration:
Secular or Religious Holiday?

Michael J. Broyde

© 2024, All Rights Reserved

ISBN: 978-1-962609-11-1

Published by The Institute for Jewish Research and Publications

Cambridge, MA

www.IJRPub.org

info@IJRPub.org

Twitter @TheIJRPub

*With Thanksgiving to the Almighty on the birth of Ella
to my daughter Rachel and son-in-law Orr Weiner
in Jerusalem, Israel on May 12, 2024 (4 Iyar, 5784)
May she be blessed with a life of joy in the Holyland*

*With Blessings to the Almighty for:
Joseph Levi Broyde
Ruth Margalit Broyde
Naomi Batya Broyde
For the joy they bring their grandfather
day in and day out, in America*

*With Gratitude to Mark Semer for his help
during the dark times more than a decade ago.
Without his assistance, all would have been lost*

Table of Contents

Preface 9

I. Introduction 11
II. The History of the American Thanksgiving 12
III. Is Thanksgiving a Secular or a Religious Holiday? .. 18
IV. A Deeper Halachic Analysis of Thanksgiving 20
    A. The Approach of Rabbi Moshe Feinstein 24
    B. The Approach of Rabbi Joseph B. Soloveitchik 30
    C. The Approach of Rabbi Yitzchak Hutner 37
    Summation of the Approaches 44
V. Further Issue Related to Celebrating Thanksgiving ... 45
VI. Conclusion 50

Introduction To Appendices I-III 53
Appendix I: Halloween 55
Appendix II: Valentine's Day 65
Appendix III: New Year's Day 71

Addendum to Appendices I-III 77
Appendix IV: Is Turkey a Kosher Bird? 79
Appendix V: Teshuva Of Rabbi Ephraim Greenblatt 85
Appendix VI: Letter From Rabbi Yitzchak Hutner 89
Appendix VII: Teshuva of Rabbi Feivel Cohen 93
Appendix VIII: Teshuva of Rabbi Yehuda Henkin 97
Appendix IX: Letter of Rabbi David Cohen 105
Appendix X: Teshuva of Rabbi Menashe Klein 113
Appendix XI
    The Complex and (Perhaps) Contradictory Approach
    or Approaches of Rabbi Moshe Feinstein Regarding
    Thanksgiving 121

Index 151
About the Author 157

יֵאָלֶה יַעַמְדוּ עַל הַבְּרָכָה

Ginzei Nistarot Society Patrons

GOLD FOUNDING PARTNER

Arielle and Donny Rosenberg

SILVER FOUNDING PARTNER

The Agus Family *(New York and Jerusalem)*

Anonymous

PATRON MEMBERS

Anonymous

Hilda and Yitz Applbaum

Nancy and Dov Friedberg

Caron and Steve Gelles

The Julis Romo Rabinowitz Family

Jennifer and Michael Kaplan

Patrons of The Ginzei Nistarot Society provide support to
The Institute for Jewish Research and Publications,
directly contributing to the growth of Jewish scholarship and fostering a deeper understanding of Judaism and its contributions to the world.

To join or to find out more information, please contact info@ijrpub.org

Preface

In 1993, I published an article titled "Thanksgiving: Secular or Religious Holiday" in volume 30 of the *Journal of Halacha and Contemporary Society*. Over the past three decades, I have been asked to expand upon its ideas to address how halacha might view other secular holidays. In response, I have added several smaller essays written over the years on related topics.

The original article referenced teshuvot by prominent Torah scholars of an earlier generation who wrote to me on this subject. Many of these responses were previously unpublished or only partially cited in the original article. In this book, I have gathered all relevant materials, either within the main text or in the appendices, and expanded the original article with additional comments from other Torah scholars.

If readers are aware of further analysis by Jewish thinkers on the celebration of secular holidays—Thanksgiving or otherwise—or have other comments, please contact me at mbroyde@emory.edu.

I am grateful to Jackson Gardner, a recent Emory College graduate and current student at Einstein Medical College, for his skilled editorial assistance, as well as to Ariel Yitzchaki, an Emory Law student, for her help with this work.

Finally, my heartfelt thanks go to my student and friend Menachem Butler, who encouraged me to expand the original article, along with subsequent essays, teshuvot sent to me, and other collected materials, into this book. Published by The Institute for Jewish Research and Publications, this work owes much to the support of both Mr. Menachem Butler and Rabbi David Shabtai, MD. I am deeply appreciative of Menachem's efforts to bring this project to publication, and I wish him success in all his endeavors.

This inaugural edition is presented with the expectation and hope of regular updates in the future. We are delighted to release it in time for Thanksgiving 2024.

I. Introduction

Thanksgiving stands as a uniquely American holiday, embraced across diverse religious and cultural communities. While some Americans incorporate personal or communal religious rituals into their observance, Thanksgiving itself has largely evolved into a secular occasion, rooted in national identity and heritage rather than specific religious traditions. This book delves into the halachic complexities surrounding the celebration of Thanksgiving,[1] analyzing whether Jewish law classifies it as a secular holiday, a religious observance, or an ambiguous blend of both.[2] Through thorough and methodical examination, it addresses the permissibility and halachic implications of various forms of Thanksgiving celebration. Additionally, the first three appendices broaden the scope to other American holidays,[3] offering a comprehensive evaluation of the halachic principles governing their observance.

---

[1] Halachic literature distinguishes between two types of "celebration" associated with Thanksgiving. The first, and most prominent, involves engaging in activities directly tied to the holiday itself, such as partaking in a festive meal with turkey and other traditional foods or participating in culturally associated events like parades. The second type of celebration is more incidental, involving the deliberate scheduling of other joyous occasions on Thanksgiving, such as weddings, to take advantage of the widespread day off from work. In fact, one of my children was married on Thanksgiving. Similarly, there is the practice in some communities of adjusting the time of the morning prayer service to a later hour, reflecting the recognition that most people are not bound by work obligations on this day.

[2] We will address the distinct controversy regarding the kosher status of turkey in Appendix IV. For the purposes of this book, we operate under the assumption that turkey is a kosher bird, consistent with the nearly universal practice within the kosher-observant community.

[3] The first appendix addresses Halloween, the second focuses on Valentine's Day, and the third examines New Year's Day. Additionally, the notes in these appendices explore the halachic considerations of other secular holidays as well

Michael J. Broyde

II. The History of the American Thanksgiving[4]

Before any halachic analysis can be done, it is necessary to place the observance of Thanksgiving in America in its proper historical context. The popular historical event, now considered the origin of the Thanksgiving Day celebration, was held in response to the survival by the pilgrims of the particularly harsh drought in 1623.[5] Not only did the colonists themselves celebrate, but food was sufficiently plentiful that

---

[4] The celebration of Canadian Thanksgiving is a different issue from that of its American counterpart. Canada celebrated its first Thanksgiving in 1578 — more than 40 years before the American Pilgrims. It was the English explorer Martin Frobisher, who held the first Thanksgiving celebration in North America, in Newfoundland. He and his crew were giving thanks for their safe return from a treacherous exploration of the Northwest Passage. Although Thanksgiving has been celebrated annually in Canada since November 6, 1879, it wasn't until 1957 when the second Monday in October (the same day as American Columbus Day) was chosen for its annual observance. There is no definitive menu for Canadian Thanksgiving and most Canadians, especially Jewish Canadians, don't even celebrate it at all. Indeed, it is an "optional holiday" in the Atlantic provinces, and it is heavily toned down in Quebec. For more on this see, Julianne Margvelashvili, "Thanksgiving, the Canadian Way," *Philadelphia Inquirer*, November 9, 1994, at section B1. See also the Wikipedia article on Thanksgiving (Canada) at https://en.wikipedia.org/wiki/Thanksgiving_(Canada) as well as "Thanksgiving in Canada in the Canadian Encyclopedia at https://www.thecanadianencyclopedia.ca/en/article/thanksgiving-day. Rabbi Mordechai Torczyner wisely noted that one reason Canadian Thanksgiving is not celebrated in the Jewish community is the fact that it often takes place during Succot. The *halachic* issues involved are thus different and not discussed by this book.

[5] Bradford, William (1952) [1620-1647]. Samuel Eliot Morison (ed.) *Of Plymouth Plantation, 1620-1647*. New York, NY: Alfred A. Knopf. pp 120-121. ISBN 978-0-394-43895-5.

even the Native Americans (with whom the colonists were at peace) were invited. This celebration took place on July 30, 1623.[6] Similar celebrations occurred throughout the New England area throughout the 1600's.[7] However, all of these were only local (rather than national or even regional) celebrations of Thanksgiving, and only occurred to mark the end of a particularly difficult winter of any given year, until 1789.[8]

In 1789, Congressman Elias Boudinot of New Jersey, proposed a resolution in Congress urging President Washington to:

> "...recommend to the people of the United States a day of public Thanksgiving and prayer to be observed by acknowledging with grateful hearts the many and signal favors of the Almighty God, especially by affording them an opportunity to establish a Constitution of government for their safety and happiness."[9]

After much debate, President Washington issued the first National Thanksgiving Proclamation, setting Thursday, November 26, 1789, as the official day of Thanksgiving and as a national holiday. Washington stated in his proclamation:

---

[6] The Pilgrims had also previously celebrated a similar, local harvest festival in 1621 at the end of their first harsh winter.

[7] One example is the Boston Thanksgiving celebration of February 22, 1630. As will be discussed below, the question of whether it would have been permissible for a Jew to join the colonists in these spontaneous celebrations is a separate issue from the permissibility of celebrating Thanksgiving in contemporary times. For more on this, see the material around pages 49 and 50 regarding the 'Thanksgiving Decree' celebrating the end of the Gulf War. Also, refer to the Wikipedia article on Thanksgiving (United States) at https://en.wikipedia.org/wiki/Thanksgiving_(United_States).

[8] This history of Thanksgiving is taken from R. & A, Linton, *We Gather Together: The Story of Thanksgiving* at pages 72-85 (1949) and from the above Wikipedia page.

[9] 1 Annals of Cong. 914 (1789).

"Now, therefore, I do recommend and assign Thursday, the 26th day of November next, to be devoted by the people of these States to the service of that great and glorious Being who is the beneficent author of all the good that was, that is, or that will be; that we may then all unite in rendering unto Him our sincere and humble thanks for His kind care and protection of the people of this country previous to their becoming a nation; for the signal and manifold mercies and the favorable interpositions of His providence in the course and conclusion of the late war; for the great degree of tranquility, union, and plenty which we have since enjoyed; for the peaceable and rational manner in which we have been enabled to establish constitutions of government for our safety and happiness, and particularly the national one now lately instituted; for the civil and religious liberty with which we are blessed, and the means we have of acquiring and diffusing useful knowledge; and, in general, for all the great and various favors which He has been pleased to confer upon us."[10]

10 See J. Richardson, *Messages and Papers of the Presidents*, 1:64. Washington continued, stating:

"And also that we may then unite in most humbly offering our prayers and supplications to the great Lord and Ruler of Nations, and beseech Him to pardon our national and other transgressions; to enable us all, whether in public or private stations, to perform our several and relative duties properly and punctually; to render our National Government a blessing to all the people by constantly being a Government of wise, just, and constitutional laws, discreetly and faithfully executed and obeyed; to protect and guide all sovereigns and nations (especially those who have shown kindness to us), and to bless them with good governments, peace, and concord; to promote the knowledge and practice of true religion and virtue, and the increase of science among them and us; and, generally, to grant

Despite the eloquence of Washington's words, and perhaps because of their overtly religious theme,[11] Thanksgiving did not become a national holiday at that time. From 1790 to 1863 there were no national celebrations of Thanksgiving. While proclamations of thanks were issued by some presidents, all the presidents for more than the next seventy years chose to ignore the day as a national holiday of Thanksgiving.[12]

> unto all mankind such a degree of temporal prosperity as He alone knows to be best."

[11] Indeed, Thomas Jefferson strongly objected to these pronouncements. He wrote:
> "Fasting and prayer are religious exercises; the enjoining them an act of discipline. Every religious society has a right to determine for itself the times for these exercises, and the objects proper for them, according to their own particular tenets; and this right can never be safer than in their own hands, where the Constitution has deposited it."

See A. Lipscomb ed., *Writings of Thomas Jefferson* 11 (1904), 429.

[12] New York State attempted to revive the holiday of Thanksgiving in 1795. However, this attempt failed because of a basic disagreement between various commercial interests over when the holiday should be celebrated. Southern states, for many years before 1846, issued Thanksgiving Day proclamations, many of which were overtly Christian, and which raised considerable protests from the Jewish community. For example:
> When James H. Hammond, governor of South Carolina, announced a day of "Thanksgiving, Humiliation, and Prayer" in 1844, he ... exhorted "our citizens of all denominations to assemble at their respective places of worship, to offer up their devotions to God their Creator, and his Son Jesus Christ, the Redeemer of the world." The Jews of Charleston protested, charging Hammond with "such obvious discrimination and preference in the tenor of your proclamation, as amounted to an utter exclusion of a portion of the people of South Carolina." Hammond responded that "I have always thought it a settled matter that I lived in a Christian land! And that I was the temporary chief magistrate of a Christian people. That in such a country and among such a people I should be, publicly, called to an account, reprimanded, and required to make amends for

It was not until 1846, when the unity of the country was again at risk due to the Missouri Compromise and the issue of slavery, that the celebration of Thanksgiving as a national holiday returned to the national agenda. From 1846 to 1863, Mrs. Sarah Josepha Hale, the editor of Godey's Lady Book,[13] embarked on a campaign to turn Thanksgiving into a national holiday during which workers would be given a day off.[14] Her campaign culminated in President Lincoln's Thanksgiving proclamation of 1863 -- the first such proclamation of a national Thanksgiving holiday since Washington's in 1789. Since 1863, Thanksgiving has been celebrated as a national holiday and a day of rest at the end of November, either on the fourth or fifth Thursday of the month.[15]

The conclusion to Lincoln's proclamation reads as follows:

> acknowledging Jesus Christ as the Redeemer of the world, I would not have believed possible, if it had not come to pass."

See M. Borden, *Jews, Turks, and Infidels* 142 n.2 (1984). Such overtly Christian proclamations have not been signed since 1860. Indeed, one is hard pressed to find in the modern era any religious celebration of Thanksgiving at all.

13 Roughly parallel to the modern *Ladies Home Journal* or *People* magazine.

14 In one of her editorials from October 1852 she wrote that "Thanksgiving Day is the national pledge of Christian faith in God, acknowledging him as the dispenser of blessings." Despite the clear Christian linkage here, her eventual letter to President Lincoln (sent on September 28, 1863) focuses on the chance to unify a broken nation underneath this holiday without any mention of Christianity. President Lincoln himself, while a deist, did not believe in being exclusively a Christian believer. See J. Zeitz *Lincoln's God: How Faith Transformed a President and a Nation* (2023) for more on this topic.

15 There has been some controversy concerning the proper date for Thanksgiving. In 1934, President Roosevelt switched the day of Thanksgiving from the last Thursday in November to the second-to-last Thursday in November when November has five weeks. This was done in an attempt to change the nation's shopping pattern and increase spending. While some objected to this mercantile approach to the holiday, Roosevelt, and mercantilism, triumphed, and since then Thanksgiving

"I do therefore invite my fellow-citizens in every part of the United States, and also those who are at sea and those who are sojourning in foreign lands, to set apart and observe the last Thursday of November next as a day of thanksgiving and praise to our beneficent Father who dwelleth in the heavens. And I recommend to them that while offering up the ascriptions justly due to Him for such singular deliverances and blessings they do also, with humble penitence for our national perverseness and disobedience, commend to His tender care all those who have become widows, orphans, mourners, or sufferers in the lamentable civil strife in which we are unavoidably engaged, and fervently implore the interposition of the Almighty hand to heal the wounds of the nation and to restore if, as soon as may be consistent with the divine purpose, to the full enjoyment of peace, harmony, tranquility, and union. In testimony whereof I have hereunto set my hand and caused the seal of the United States to be affixed. Done at the city of Washington, this 3rd day of October A.D. 1863, and of the Independence of the United States the eighty-eighth." [16]

---

has been celebrated in the second to last week of November (when it has five Thursdays).

[16] President Lincoln's full Proclamation:

"The year that is drawing toward its close has been filled with the blessings of fruitful fields and healthful skies. To these bounties, which are so constantly enjoyed that we are prone to forget the source from which they come, others have been added which are of so extraordinary a nature that they cannot fail to penetrate and soften even the heart which is habitually insensible to the ever-watchful providence of Almighty God. In the midst of a civil war of unequaled magnitude and severity, which has sometimes seemed to foreign states to invite and to provoke their aggression, peace has

Michael J. Broyde

III. Is Thanksgiving a Secular or a Religious Holiday?

The first major point that must be addressed before permitting Jews to celebrate Thanksgiving, is to classify it as either a secular or religious holiday. Today, Thanksgiving is typically classified by American law as a secular, national holiday. One might ask whether halacha should simply defer to this American legal classification. In fact, once this conclusion is reached, it can be argued that little controversy remains. The simple answer, however, is that American law adopts a definition of "secular" that is clearly "religious" in the eyes of halacha. For example, in Cammack v. Waihee,[17] a court determined that the holiday called "Good

> been preserved with all nations, order has been maintained, the laws have been respected and obeyed, and harmony has prevailed everywhere, except in the theater of military conflict, while that theater has been greatly contracted by the advancing armies and navies of the Union. Needful diversions of wealth and of strength from the fields of peaceful industry to the national defense have not arrested the plow, the shuttle, or the ship; the ax has enlarged the borders of our settlements, and the mines, as well of iron and coal as of the precious metals, have yielded even more abundantly than heretofore. Population has steadily increased notwithstanding the waste that has been made in the camp, the siege, and the battlefield, and the country, rejoicing in the consciousness of augmented strength and vigor, is permitted to expect continuance of years with large increase of freedom. No human counsel hath devised nor hath any mortal hand worked out these great things. They are the gracious gifts of the Most High God, who, while dealing with us in anger for our sins, hath nevertheless remembered mercy. It has seemed to me fit and proper that they should be solemnly, reverently, and gratefully acknowledged, as with one heart and one voice, by the whole American people....."

[17] 673 F.Supp. 1524 (D. Haw. 1987).

Friday" was a "secular" holiday. So too, the Supreme Court has ruled that both Christmas and Chanuka are "secular" holidays and have "secular" displays that lack a religious theme.[18] Certainly, halacha views none of these as "secular" and thus would not accept American law's definition of "secular" as halachically binding.[19] Hence, American law cannot be relied upon to determine which holidays are "secular" and which are "religious."

Rather, to give Thanksgiving a halachic definition of secular, the first question is whether Thanksgiving has roots in a clearly pagan or Christian celebration that is held for the purpose of promoting their unique religious theology. As shown above, the many local "Thanksgiving" celebrations were performed with the intent of showing thanks for the survival of a harsh winter, or other difficulty, which allowed for a successful harvest season. These were not held as pagan celebrations, nor were they comprised of promoting uniquely Christian values, but rather were intended to thank "the Almighty" who guided their harvest.[20] As noted above, even Washington's national declaration which mentioned this thanks to "the Almighty," received pushback from figures such as Thomas Jefferson, who viewed any religious reference as being improper. All official declarations of the holiday have at most, only contained a general religious character, which could apply to many different faiths.

The second question is whether Thanksgiving is currently celebrated as a religious holiday. It is quite clear that today the overwhelming majority of Americans view Thanksgiving as a day off from work in which they can enjoy the theme of gratitude for their lives while enjoying a nice

---

[18] *Lynch v. Donnelly*, 465 U.S. 668 (1984); *Allegheny v. American Civil Liberties Union*, 492 U.S. 573 (1989).

[19] This is noted quite clearly by Rabbi Menashe Klein, *Mishneh Halachot* 10:116, discussed infra., and translated in Appendix X.

[20] It is significant that references to "the Almighty" in Thanksgiving literature do not mention concepts such as the trinity, which *halacha* would view as more problematic.

family meal, and perhaps a parade or a sports game. There is no explicitly theological message or ritualistic purpose behind these acts; it is viewed no differently than celebrating a holiday such as Independence Day (in contrast, for example to Christmas, which is also a federal holiday).

IV. A Deeper Halachic Analysis of Thanksgiving

Having reviewed the history of Thanksgiving, and having halachically defined it as a secular holiday, it is now necessary to turn to the question of whether there are still further halachic issues involved in its "celebration." The first, and most significant issue, is whether it is permissible to eat a Thanksgiving meal with the classical foods that American tradition dictates that one should eat at this meal, namely, turkey and cranberry sauce, or if this is a forbidden form of "imitating Gentile customs." Among the authorities of the previous generation, three different positions have been taken on this topic, and these three positions have each been accepted by various Jewish communities in our generation.

However, before these three positions can be understood, some background into the nature of the prohibition against imitating Gentile customs is in order.[21] Maimonides states:

> "We may not follow the statutes of the [Gentiles] or resemble them in their [style] of dress, hair, or the like, as [Leviticus 20:23] states: "In the statutes of the

[21] For an in-depth elaboration on this issue, see Rabbi Tzvi Teichman, "The Jew in a Gentile Society: *Chukat Ha'akum*," *Journal of Halacha and Contemporary Society*, vol. 3 (1981): 64-85. For a fine review of the primary sources in this issue, see "*Chukat Akum*" in the *Halachipedia* article at https://halachipedia.com/index.php?title=Chukot_Akum and Rabbi Yechiel Yaakov Weinberg, *Seridei Eish* 2:39.

nation [that I am driving out before you], do not walk," as [Leviticus 18:3] states: "in their statutes you will not walk," and as [Deuteronomy 12:30] states: "Be careful, lest you inquire after them."

[All these verses] share a single topic: they warn us not to try to resemble [the Gentiles]. Instead, the Jews should be separate from them and distinct in their dress and in their deeds, as they are in their ideals and character traits. In this context, [Leviticus 20:26] states: "I have separated you from the nations [to be Mine]."

[Thus,] one may not wear a garment which is unique to them or grow the corners of our hair as they do. We may not shave our heads from the sides and leave hair in the center as they do. This is called a blorit. We may not shave the hair on the front of our faces from ear to ear and leave a growth at the back of our heads as they do... Whoever performs one of the above or a deed of this nature is [liable for] lashes.[22]

It emerges from Maimonides' codification, that the Jewish people must keep themselves distinct from the other nations and must avoid any practices with which the Gentiles distinguish themselves. This exact formulation of Maimonides was then codified by Rabbi Karo in the Shulchan Aruch.[23] While the above codification lists a few examples, other poskim more explicitly define what customs fall under this prohibition.

Tosafot teaches that two distinctly different categories of customs are forbidden under the prohibition against imitating Gentile customs. The first is "idolatrous customs" and the second is "foolish customs"

---

[22] *Mishneh Torah, The Laws of Idolatry,* Chapter 11:1.

[23] *Shulchan Aruch,* YD 178:1.

even if their origins are not idolatrous.[24] Ran and Maharik disagree, and rule that only customs that have their origins in idolatrous practices are forbidden. Seemingly foolish, secular customs are permissible so long as they have a reasonable explanation (and are not immodest).[25] According to all approaches however, the purpose of the prohibition against imitating Gentile customs is, as mentioned above, to ensure that the Jews remain distinct and do not assimilate into Gentile culture.[26] Rema codified the normative halacha as following the ruling of Ran and Maharik:

> "Those practices done as a [Gentile] custom or law with no reason to suspect that it is an idolatrous practice or that there are idolatrous origins [are permitted]…Customs which are practiced for a reason, such as the physician who wears a special garment to identify himself as a doctor, may be practiced…the same is true for any custom done out of honor or any other reason is permissible."[27]

---

[24] Tosafot, *Avodah Zarah* 11a s.v. *ve'ei*. Tosafot, and all other authorities discussed in this section, are resolving a tension between the *Talmudic* passage here and the one in *Sanhedrin* 52b.

[25] Ran, *Avodah Zarah* 11a s.v. *yisrael*; *Chidushei HaRan*, *Sanhedrin* 52b; Maharik, Responsa 58. This position seems to contradict the position of Maimonides and *Shulchan Aruch*, who do not distinguish between categories of customs; they would perhaps support Tosafot instead in forbidding even secular customs. For more on this, see *Sefer Yeraim Siman* 313, Rabbi Yechiel Yaakov Weinberg, *Seridei Eish* 2:39 and *Igrot Moshe YD* 4:11. See also *Mesorat Moshe* 2: page 196 on wearing graduation gowns. I once asked Rabbi Aharon Lichenstein about this last topic, and he did not think it was a real problem since these are worn to identify the graduates and are like a doctor's uniform.

[26] *Chinuch* 262.

[27] Rema, *YD* 178:1.

As will be seen later, there are authorities who favor being strict, in accordance with the opinion of the Gaon of Vilna (Gra), who rules that the only time secular customs are permissible to be practiced is when they have a Jewish origin.[28] According to this approach, secular customs created by Gentiles are prohibited even when their origins are not religious. However, this is not the normative halacha.

Additionally, independent of the halachic obligation to avoid Gentile religious customs, it goes without saying that it is forbidden for a Jew to celebrate idolatrous religious events himself. Thus, a Jew may not attend an idolatrous "Indian"[29] office party or directly facilitate its observance.[30] So too, a Jew may not attend a birthday party for an idol worshipper if the birthday party includes the worship of idols, even though celebrating a birthday party is itself not problematic.[31]

It is also worth mentioning that closely related to the ban on imitating Gentile customs and practices, is a category of forbidden practices known

---

[28] Gra, *YD* 178:7. This stricture is based on Tosafot's argument from *Avodah Zarah* 11a where the category of "foolish customs" are forbidden: Tosafot mentions within this category the idea that if the *Torah* had written (or perhaps alluded) to these foolish practices then, despite Gentiles practicing them, they would nevertheless have been permitted. For a review of the authorities who disagree with Gra, see *Seridei Eish* 2:39 and 2:40.

[29] For a discussion on why halacha refers to "Indian" practices when discussing idolatry, see the * footnote in the second edition of the *Mishnah Berurah* in 330:8 (which is commonly deleted in modern reprintings). See also the prefatory remarks of Rabbi Chaim Cohen in *Divrei Geonim*, and the extremely illuminating remarks of Rabbi Bleich on "self-censorship" and avoidance of "imposed censorship" found in Rabbi J. David Bleich, "Extraditing Jews," *Techumin* 8:297, 301-302 (5747).

[30] *YD* 147:6-9. The issue of how much assistance is permissible in cases where the violation will occur whether or not the Jew assists is beyond the scope of this book. For more on that, see my **"Assisting in a Violation of Noachide Law"** Published in: *Jewish Law Association Studies VIII: The Jerusalem 1994 Conference Volume* (1996), 11–20.

[31] *YD* 147:4-7.

as "darchei emori," (the ways of the Emorites). This category of forbidden practices consists of ancient Gentile superstitions, such as wearing a red string around one's finger, uttering special incantations when encountering certain animals, and throwing stones into a pond, among others.[32] It is forbidden for a Jew to practice any darchei emori customs, although some authorities allow an exception when it is for healing purposes.[33] For the most part, the issues of darchei emori are not relevant when debating the permissibility of observing American secular holidays. Now that these halachic topics have been clarified, it is time to discuss the three major approaches to celebrating Thanksgiving Day.

A. *The Approach of Rabbi Moshe Feinstein*

Rabbi Moshe Feinstein has four published responsa (teshuvot) on the issues related to celebrating Thanksgiving, all of which conclude that Thanksgiving is a secular holiday, not a religious one. The first teshuva, written in 1953/5723, discusses the deliberate scheduling of weddings, and the like, on religious holidays of other faiths. Rabbi Feinstein states:

> "On the question of celebrating an event on a holiday of the Gentiles: if the holiday is based on religious beliefs [by the Gentiles] [then] such celebrations are prohibited according to [Jewish] law if deliberately scheduled on that day; even without intent, it is prohibited because of marit ayin[34] ...

---

[32] *Tosefta* (Lieberman Edition), *Shabbat* 6:1.

[33] *Shabbat* 67a; OC 301:27.

[34] Marit ayin is a term used to describe actions that might appear to onlookers as a transgression. A classic example of marit ayin is eating or drinking kosher food in a non-kosher restaurant. Similarly, when non-dairy creamer and 'kosher cheeseburgers' first appeared, they raised serious concerns about marit ayin. Nowadays, however, these foods have become mainstream, and consuming them no longer arouses such suspicions. Issues of marit ayin change and evolve

Jewish Law and the American Thanksgiving Celebration

The first day of their year [January 1],[35] and Thanksgiving are not prohibited according to the law, but pious people [baalei nefesh] should be strict [not to do so]."[36]

Rabbi Feinstein reinforces his understanding that Thanksgiving is not a religious holiday in a teshuva published in 1980/5741. He states:

"On the issue of joining with those who think that Thanksgiving is like a holiday to make a meal: since it is clear that according to their religious law books this day is not mentioned as a religious holiday, and that one is not obligated in a meal [according to Gentile religious law], and since this is [only] a day of remembrance for the citizens of this country [for] when they came to reside here…halacha sees no prohibition in celebrating with a

with social norms, driven by when something is reasonably misunderstood as something else.

[35] The status of New Year's Day has changed in the last hundred years. In contemporary America there is little religious content or expression to New Year's Day, and while there might be many problems associated with the way some celebrate it, few would classify it as a religious holiday. However, Terumat HaDeshen 195, writing nearly five hundred years ago, classifies New Year's as a religious holiday. This is quoted by Rema, *YD* 148:12. Terumat HaDeshen discusses whether one may give a New Year's Day gift and refers to January 1st as "the eighth day of Christmas." He clearly understands the holiday as religious in nature and covered by the prohibition of assisting a Gentile in his worship. (The text of the common edition of the *Shulchan Aruch* here has undoubtedly been subject to considerable censorship. For an accurate rendition of Rema, see Rema's *Darchei Moshe* in the recent edition of the *Tur* published by *Machon Yerushalyim*.). This is perhaps why Rabbi Feinstein in the calendar for *Ezrat Torah* does not list New Year's Day since that calendar was made in the 1930's when New Year's Day was more religious while this teshuva from the 1950's already was in a more secular society. For more on this, see Appendix III.

[36] *Igrot Moshe*, EH 2:13. Rabbi Feinstein's view is explained in much more textual detain in Appendix XI.

> meal or with the eating of turkey. One sees similarly in Kiddushin 66a where we read that King Yannai made a celebration after the conquest of Kochalit in the desert and they [the Sages] ate vegetables as a remembrance.
>
> Nonetheless, it is prohibited to establish this as an obligation and religious commandment [mitzvah]…it must remain a voluntary celebration…in this manner -- without the establishment of obligation or religious commandment -- one can celebrate the next year too with a meal. But, I think nonetheless, it is prohibited to establish a fixed day in the year for the celebration [of Thanksgiving] since it [was] only in the first year of the event, when Yannai conquered [Kochalit], that they had a celebration, and [they did] not [do so] permanently [every year]. There is also a [problem] of "adding commandments [to those already in the Torah]…"[37] Even though one can question the source [of adding anything to the Torah], it is still a real prohibition."[38]

Thus, Rabbi Feinstein appears to also rule here that Thanksgiving is not a religious holiday, and there is no prohibition of celebrating "Gentile holidays" while observing it. Nonetheless, he prohibits its ongoing celebration as an obligation on a particular day because he feels that this would be a prohibited addition to the Jewish calendar and would create a problem of adding commandments to the Torah (baal tosif). While Rabbi Feinstein's objections to adding observances will be discussed later, it is clear that he sees no problem in Thanksgiving's celebration as

---

[37] Rabbi Feinstein cites *Megillah* 7a and Nachmanides (Ramban) regarding *Deuteronomy* 4:2.

[38] *Igrot Moshe*, YD 4:11:4.

a Gentile holiday, and he appears to see no problem with eating a turkey meal on that day as a matter of choice, and not obligation.[39]

As proof to the fact that Rabbi Feinstein rules that eating turkey is permissible,[40] he states elsewhere in the same teshuva:

> "Thus, it is obvious in my opinion, that even [in a case] where something would be considered a prohibited Gentile custom, if the general populace of Gentiles do it for reasons unrelated to their religion or law, but rather because it is pleasurable to them, then already there is no prohibition of imitating Gentile customs. So too, it is obvious that if Gentiles were to make a religious law to eat a particular item that is good to eat, halacha would not prohibit eating that item. So too, any item of pleasure in the world cannot be prohibited merely because Gentiles do so out of religious observance."[41]

However, in another teshuva (also written in 1980/5741), Rabbi Feinstein seems to state that, in fact, there is a prohibition against celebrating Thanksgiving, even though he acknowledges that

---

[39] Thus, for example, this author suspects that Rabbi Feinstein would feel it not problematic to note Thanksgiving -- like Labor Day, Independence Day, and Memorial Day are noted -- on synagogue calendars as a secular holiday. Indeed, Thanksgiving Day (along with Columbus Day, Veterans Day, Election Day, Presidents Day, Memorial Day, Independence Day, and Labor Day) are all noted in the 1930's *Ezrat Torah* calendar which was published under Rabbi Feinstein's (and Rabbi Yosef Eliyahu Henkin's) auspices. (New Year's Day and Christmas Day are not.) So too, I suspect that Rabbi Feinstein would permit teaching school children about Thanksgiving as part of their general studies curriculum just as he would permit Columbus and Columbus Day to be discussed.

[40] See Appendix IV where this is noted as the common practice.

[41] Rabbi Feinstein then applies this principle to going bare-headed, and rules that even if some Gentiles do so out of religious fervor, since many people do so out of concerns for comfort, this is not considered a religious custom.

Thanksgiving lacks religious content. In this teshuva, he views such celebratory activity on Thanksgiving as irrational and, therefore, prohibited as a form of imitating secular society.[42] In his fourth teshuva,[43] Rabbi Feinstein clarifies that this stance is essentially a stringency,[44] as it assumes that even secular rituals without religious origins are forbidden. Indeed, in this teshuva, he emphasizes[45] that the earlier view quoted above should be considered the normative one.

Rabbi Ephraim Greenblatt, a prominent student of Rabbi Feinstein, also permits the celebration of Thanksgiving with the eating of turkey.[46] He writes that he has a teshuva,[47] where he rules that it is permissible to eat turkey on Thanksgiving because Thanksgiving is "only a day of thanks, and not, heaven forbid, for idol worship." Rabbi Greenblatt adds that he posed this question more than thirty years ago to Rabbi Eliezer Silver and that Rabbi Silver also ruled that it was permissible to

---

[42] *Igrot Moshe*, OC 5:20:6. However, a close examination of this letter reveals that the only time Rabbi Feinstein would consider such conduct prohibited is if it was done with celebratory rituals associated with celebrating Thanksgiving, perhaps reciting a text or singing a song, and not merely eating a family meal. It is interesting to note that in 2013 *Hallel* was recited on Thanksgiving (with a blessing!) since it coincided with *Chanuka*. This overlap will occur again in 2070.

[43] *Igrot Moshe*, YD 4:12. This final *teshuva* was written in response to Rabbi Feinstein's grandson Rabbi Tendler, who noted that the analyses found in *Igrot Moshe*, OC 5:20:6, *Igrot Moshe*, YD 4:11:4, and *Igrot Moshe*, EH 2:13 seemed to be at tension with one another. Indeed, it should be noted that Rabbi Feinstein repeatedly ruled that secular customs that have no religious origins are permissible. For a more in-depth discussion on Rabbi Feinstein's contradictory *teshuvot*, see Appendix XI.

[44] See the Introduction to this section where Tosafot, the Gra, and perhaps even Maimonides and *Shulchan Aruch* consider such a practice forbidden.

[45] *Igrot Moshe* YD 4:11:4

[46] Found in Appendix V in a letter to this author, dated August 5754.

[47] In his *Rivevot Ephraim* series. This *teshuva* was never published to the best of my knowledge and is only found in Appendix V.

eat turkey on Thanksgiving.[48] Nevertheless, as we will see below, Rabbi David Cohen, and likely others, does not explicitly forbid celebrating Thanksgiving but does frown upon participating in the custom of eating turkey, arguing that it is "irrational," and, therefore, forbidden.

Meanwhile, Rabbi Yisroel Belsky's opinion somewhat resembles his teacher Rabbi Feinstein's more reserved approach. He writes: "Regarding the Thanksgiving holiday: if such parties were made as a sign of patriotism to the United States, it would be acceptable for Jews to make them as well as a sign of loyalty to their host country. This does not seem to be the case however, and there is no reason that a Jew should make them."[49] Essentially, Rabbi Belsky argues that a Thanksgiving celebration is permitted, but since the day has moved from positive values such as patriotism to just football and shopping, there are no positive religious reasons to celebrate and no concerns (seeming to be unpatriotic) not to celebrate. Thus, there is no reason to celebrate Thanksgiving even if such celebrations are not prohibited.

B. *The Approach of Rabbi Joseph B. Soloveitchik*

Rabbi Joseph B. Soloveitchik[50] also agreed that Thanksgiving was not a Gentile holiday and ruled that it was permissible to eat turkey on

---

[48] It is also clear from Rabbi Greenblatt's letter that he feels that Rabbi Feinstein agrees with his ruling, see Appendix V. Only Rabbi Menashe Klein disagreed with Rabbi Greenblatt, see *Mishneh Halachot* 10:116 found in Appendix X for his full response to Rabbi Greenblatt.

[49] See *Piskei Halacha* of Rabbi Belsky, Compiled by Rabbi Moishe Dovid Lebovits at pages 163-164. (Rabbi Yisroel Belsky (1938-2016) was the senior *Kashrut* advisor for the Orthodox Union and the *Rosh Yeshiva* of *Torah Vodaas*.). In 1995 I spoke to Rabbi Belsky at some length about this and he adopted the view in conversation that maybe even Rabbi Soloveitchik would agree with his view in 1995.

[50] Rabbi Dr. Joseph B. Soloveitchik (1903-1993) was the *rosh yeshiva* at Yeshiva University from 1941 until his passing. He held a PhD from the University of

Thanksgiving. As Rabbi Hershel Schachter writes in his intellectual biography of Rabbi Soloveitchik, *Nefesh HaRav*:

> "It was the opinion of Rabbi Soloveitchik that it was permissible to eat turkey at the end of November, on Thanksgiving. We understood that, in his opinion, there was no question that turkey is a kosher bird[51] and that eating it on Thanksgiving was not a problem of imitating gentile customs. We also heard that this was the opinion of his father, Rabbi Moshe Soloveitchik."[52]

Others have also reported that Rabbi Soloveitchik ruled this way, and that he found it difficult to comprehend how one could consider Thanksgiving a Gentile holiday or rule that it is forbidden to celebrate it.[53] Indeed, there were instances when Rabbi Soloveitchik implied to his

---

Berlin and gave a widely admired and highly conceptual *Talmud* class at YU, all the while living in Boston.

51 For more on this issue, see Appendix IV.

52 For the Hebrew text from *Nefesh HaRav*, 231:

חוקת עכו"ם: [א] דעת רבנו היתה שמותר לאכול בשר הודו (טורקי) בסוף נובמבר ביום טקסגיוויינג, והבינינו שלדעתו אין בבשר הודו בעיא של חסרון מסורה [נ"ע ליקוט דברי הפוסקים בזה בדרכ"ת ליו"ד סי' פ"ב], וכן שאין באכילתם ביום טקסגיוויינג משום חוקות הגוים. וכן שמעתי גם דעת אביו הגרמ"ס ז"ל.

53 Rabbi Howard (Chaim) Jachter of Teaneck noted to me that he spoke to Rabbi Soloveitchik about this in July 1985 and that Rabbi Soloveitchik affirmed this ruling and did not see any problem with celebrating Thanksgiving. Dr. Avi Feldblum also confirmed to this author that he heard such a ruling from Rabbi Soloveitchik. Dr. Marc Shapiro of University of Scranton wrote to me: "I asked the Rav if there was anything wrong with celebrating Thanksgiving and he, very surprised, responded, "What could be wrong about celebrating Thanksgiving[?]" I responded that I had heard that a certain rabbi had claimed that since the holiday had a religious origin therefore it was forbidden for Jews to mark the day. The Rav asked me: "Do you plan on going to church on that day?" I replied in the negative

students that he and his family celebrated Thanksgiving, although his shiur was always held on Thanksgiving.[54]

Indeed, Rabbi Soloveitchik would explicitly mention his Thanksgiving celebrations sometimes. Rabbi Aaron Rakeffet-Rothkoff recounts:

> "The Rav used to come in from Boston Tuesday morning, said shiur at 1:00 in the afternoon, and then again at 10:00 Wednesday morning. One year he couldn't come in Tuesday because of a wedding in Boston, so he came in Wednesday. After he finished shiur on Wednesday, he looked at his watch and said, "Tomorrow, we'll say the shiur at 9:00, will you be here?" I said, "Rebbe, we'll be there, but why so early?" So the Rav looked at me: "Arnold,

and the Rav continued: "So what then is the problem[?]" This dialogue with Rabbi Soloveitchik mimics Rabbi Henkin's observation that even if a secular holiday is religiously celebrated by some, that is not a concern.

[54] Dr. Avi Feldblum recounted:
> While I do not know whether Rabbi Soloveitchik had turkey for dinner that night or whether he called it a Thanksgiving dinner, it was well known that on Thanksgiving, Rav Soloveitchik started *shiur* much earlier than usual in order to end earlier and be able to catch a plane back to Boston to have a festive meal etc. However, it is of interest to note that while Thanksgiving appeared to be of sufficient importance to change the fixed start time for *shiur*, it was not sufficient to end *shiur* earlier if the Rav had not completed what he wanted to teach. On Thanksgiving 1976, there was the famous Thanksgiving *shiur* where the Rav spent about five hours (most of it in silent thought) working through one Tosafot. After the second or third time the *shamash* passed him a note about the flight [back to Boston], the Rav turned to him and said, "no one can leave here until we have understood what it is that Tosafot is saying!"

Letter of Dr. Avi Feldblum, published electronically in mail.jewish, volume 5, issue 20 available in archives at mail-jewish@shamash.nysernet.org don't you understand? Tomorrow's Thanksgiving. We have Thanksgiving dinner with my sister, and I promised my wife we'll be there at 2:00. So I have to catch the 12:00 plane."[55]

Rabbi Soloveitchik's model of encouraging the celebration of Thanksgiving is grounded less in patriotism and more in gratitude. It recognizes that America and the government of the United States of America have been good to the Jews and that we ought to have a sense of gratefulness for that. Thanksgiving is the time to express that sense of thanks.[56] Rabbi Norman Lamm, one of Rabbi Soloveitchik's leading students, expresses this idea during a Thanksgiving sermon. He stated:

> "The Thanksgiving Day Services at the Spanish-Portuguese Synagogue are not only a fine patriotic gesture as loyal American citizens; they are also an authentic expression of Judaism.[57] In the same sense, when our

---

[55] Rabbi Aaron Rakeffet Rothkoff "From Lakewood to Yeshiva University" at http://matzav.com/from-lakewood-to-yeshiva-university/. He would end this story by noting "I had never celebrated Thanksgiving. I was a *kana'i* [fanatic] like most kids. When I came home and told my mother the story, she was in ecstasy. She said to me, "Why can't you be modern like Rav Soloveitchik?"

[56] As noted earlier, while Rabbi Belsky agrees with these ideas, he also feels that today Thanksgiving celebrations have moved away from these values and thus Jews have no reason to celebrate anymore. It would seem that the students of Rabbi Soloveitchik, who uphold his rulings on Thanksgiving, might agree with Rabbi Belsky that most don't celebrate with these values anymore, but that Jews must nevertheless continue expressing these forgotten values to educate their families on them, and to serve as examples of proper behavior.

[57] Rabbi Lamm delivered this sermon at Congregation *Shearith Israel*, one of the oldest Sephardic communities in America. This congregation has historic ties to Thanksgiving which date to Washington's National Thanksgiving Proclamation in 1789, which spurred their hazzan and religious leader, Gershom Mendes Seixas, to deliver a Thanksgiving address of his own to the synagogue. In this address he

fellow Americans repair each to his own house of worship to offer thanks to our Heavenly Father for the blessings of life, freedom, peace, and bounty which we enjoy in our beloved land, we Jews feel quite naturally obliged to turn to God and, in our own way, to thank Him. *** Yet it is not enough merely to approve of Thanksgiving Day. Judaism has, as well, an original approach to the phenomenon of gratitude that is analytic and profound in nature, and in which there is implicit a remarkable spiritual insight. Obviously our thanks are not made to flatter God. What then does the Torah tradition mean when it emphasizes the importance of thanking Him?

It is this thoroughly Jewish idea — the dual nature of hodayah and the inexorable failure and mortal danger of human ways without God that should be our specific Jewish contribution to the American experience of Thanksgiving. It is for this reason that, to my mind, Thanksgiving Day is so much more precious than other national holidays. Other patriotic occasions, such as Independence Day, valuable though they are, can easily degenerate into national self-idolatry and collective self-glorification. In order to reestablish the proper harmony we need the kind of corrective of humility inspired by Thanksgiving Day. For if July 4th is Independence

---

states, "As Jews, we are even more than others, called upon to return thanks to God for placing us in such a country – where we are free to act according to the dictates of conscience, and where no exception is taken from following the principles of our religion." Seixas' address resembles both Rabbi Soloveitchik's and Rabbi Lamm's messages of expressing gratitude for the freedoms and benefits that Jews receive in America. It is interesting to note that *Shearith Israel* has not had special Thanksgiving services since the early 1970s (according to its rabbi at that time, Rabbi Marc Angel, by email to me) reflecting the social changes in the nature of Thanksgiving that Rabbi Belsky mentions.

Day, then Thanksgiving is our Dependence Day — our dependence upon the Almighty.

For all this we thank You, O Lord. And even as during the rest of the year we pray "God, bless America," today we turn to our own hearts and to the soul of our country and declare, "America, bless God."[58]

A similar view is also taken by Rabbi Yehuda Herzl Henkin, who states that the celebration of Thanksgiving is based on Torah concepts and that it is clear that halacha does not consider Thanksgiving to be a religious holiday. He says that even if one lived in a society where some religious denominations celebrate Thanksgiving "religiously," that would not be sufficient to make it a religious holiday, as it is clear that many secular people celebrate it.[59] Nevertheless, Rabbi Henkin

---

[58] Rabbi Norman Lamm's Thanksgiving Sermon (1962) is available through OU Press: https://oupress.org/excerpts/thanksgiving-sermon-lamm/. The full text can also be accessed via the Yeshiva University Archives: https://archives.yu.edu/gsdl/collect/lammserm/index/assoc/HASH0126.dir/doc.pdf. In this sermon, Rabbi Lamm emphasizes the positive values of Thanksgiving, aligning with the perspective Rabbi Belsky endorsed, reflecting the era's broader embrace of the holiday. For similar examples, see Janet Linker's The Last Verse for Thanksgiving and Patriotic Celebrations (published by Beckkeyboard Press) or Rabbi Joseph Lookstein's Thanksgiving Prayer from 1940. The program for the Thanksgiving Service at Congregation Kehilath Jeshurun, held on Thursday, November 21, 1940, at 11:00 a.m., is available at https://kavvanah.blog/wp-content/uploads/2014/11/thanksgiving-service-at-kj-1940-edited.pdf (curated by Alan Brill). Another notable example is the 1945 Thanksgiving Service by Rabbi David de Sola Pool at Congregation Shearith Israel, accessible at https://kavvanah.blog/wp-content/uploads/2009/11/thanksgiving-service-pool.pdf (also curated by Alan Brill).

[59] This argument centers on the permissibility of observing customs and practices rooted in secular origins. While the Vilna Gaon (the *Gra*) rules such practices as forbidden, normative halacha does not appear to adopt his stringent stance. For a more in-depth analysis, see *Bnei Banim* 2:30.

suggests that one should occasionally skip the Thanksgiving meal as a way of indicating that it is not a religious obligation but merely optional in nature. This would accommodate the stricture of Rabbi Feinstein.[60] Rabbi Henkin concludes:

> "...We have [no source] to prohibit rejoicing on the king's birthday and [during] similar events? The practices of the Jewish people throughout the generations proves [there is no such prohibition]. Rather, [we must conclude that] there are two separate laws. On a [Gentile] religious holiday, it is prohibited to purchase from and sell to Gentiles since they offer sacrifices to idolatrous deities [on that day]. [Regarding] this [rule], it is of no relevance to us what the reason [behind the establishment] of the holiday is. Even the [coronation] day of the king and his birthday are prohibited [if celebrated religiously]... But regarding that which was established based on other considerations, and the holiday is primarily of a civil nature, it is permitted to celebrate on it, examples being the [coronation] day of the king, or the Fourth of July in the United States and Thanksgiving. Regarding this [latter category of secular celebrations], it is of no relevance to us that [some] Gentiles worship their deity specifically on those days as well."[61]

---

[60] Notably, Rabbi Henkin respects Rabbi Feinstein's caution regarding Thanksgiving but takes a different approach. Rabbi Feinstein permits Thanksgiving celebrations reluctantly, viewing them as essentially purposeless and advising pious individuals to refrain. Rabbi Henkin, however, aligns more closely with Rabbi Soloveitchik, seeing intrinsic Torah values in Thanksgiving and encouraging its celebration as an expression of gratitude. For Rabbi Henkin's full letter, see Appendix VIII, and for a detailed discussion of Rabbi Feinstein's position, see Appendix XI.

[61] Rabbi Henkin, in his letter dated 23 Tevet 5755 (published in *Bnei Banim* 3:37 and reproduced in full in Appendix VIII), states that it is permissible to adjust

Rabbi Henkin, however, offers one significant caveat. As stated in the Shulchan Aruch, it is clearly prohibited to join in the celebration of even a completely secular holiday—such as the coronation of a king[62]—if Gentiles are marking that day with pagan or religious observances.[63] In contrast, joining Gentiles in a purely secular celebration of Thanksgiving, as most Americans do, is permissible.[64] Therefore, even those authorities who permit observing Thanksgiving with a meal would not allow doing so alongside Gentiles who are celebrating it with religious intent. (This principle similarly applies to secular occasions like a birthday party, wedding,[65] or funeral.

    the time of morning services on Thanksgiving, acknowledging that many people are off from work. However, for a legal holiday with religious significance for Gentiles—such as December 25—he advises disregarding the holiday entirely when scheduling services. In contrast, Rabbi David Cohen advises against altering the time of prayer services even on a regular Sunday and considers it especially inappropriate to make adjustments on a Gentile holiday. For further details on Rabbi David Cohen's stance, see his letter dated 9 Nissan 5755 in Appendix IX.

62 Notably, commemorating the death of a king may also be prohibited, and conducting business with Gentiles on such a day may likewise be forbidden. See Mishnah, Avodah Zarah 8a.

63 *YD* 148:6.

64 *YD* 148:5. See also comments of *Beit Yosef* on *Tur, YD* 148 s.v. *ubegoy shemakirin be she'ano oved avodah zarah, hakol mutar.*

65 It is worth noting that attending a pagan wedding may be categorically forbidden, and even those who permit attending generally prohibit partaking in the celebratory meal—even if the food is entirely kosher. See Avodah Zarah 8a and Yoreh Deah 152:1. Igrot Moshe (*YD* 2:117) permits attendance when concerns of eiva (arousing animosity toward Jews) are relevant, following the opinion of Shach, who classifies the prohibition as rabbinic and therefore allows leniency in cases of eiva. Mishneh Halachot 7:118, however, adopts a stringent position, aligning with Taz, who views the prohibition as biblical, thus negating leniency on the grounds of eiva. There may, however, be grounds to permit attendance at a Muslim wedding

C. The Approach of Rabbi Yitzchak Hutner

An exactly opposite approach to the rulings of Rabbis Feinstein and Soloveitchik appears to have been taken by Rabbi Yitzchak Hutner.[66] Rabbi Hutner argues that it is obvious that, whatever the merit of celebrating the first Thanksgiving in the 1600s was, the establishment of an annual holiday that is based on the Christian calendar is, at the very least, closely associated with idol worship and thus prohibited.[67] Rabbi

---

(where the concept of God is strictly monotheistic) or possibly at a completely secular ceremony. For further discussion, see Yabia Omer 10, Yoreh Deah 13.

[66] Rabbi Yitzchak Hutner, *Pachad Yitzchak: Igrot uMichtavim shel HaRav Hutner* (5751), 109, as reproduced in Appendix VI, is cited in the context of Thanksgiving. However, the term "appears" is used deliberately, as the title suggests Rabbi Hutner addresses Thanksgiving, yet the letter itself was not authored by him. Since the volume was published posthumously, it is possible the letter pertains to a different occasion. Supporting this interpretation, Rabbi David Cohen (of Congregation Gvul Yavetz) recalls:

> "I once heard from my teacher, Rabbi Yitzchak Hutner, that he saw no prohibition in eating turkey on Thanksgiving. On the contrary, he viewed it positively, as the Gentiles act out of a sense of gratitude—a concept harmonious with Jewish values (based on Talmud, Menachot 73b, [s.v.] akum lebo leshamayim...)."

For the full text of Rabbi Cohen's letter, dated 9 Nissan 5755, see Appendix XI.

[67] Rabbi Hutner astutely noted that the Gregorian calendar has its origins in Christian theology, as it was designed to ensure the accurate annual timing of Easter. The use of terms like B.C. ("Before Christ") and A.D. (Anno Domini, meaning "The Year of Our Lord") to denote years further underscores its Christian orientation. However, beginning in the 17th century with Johannes Kepler, alternative designations such as B.C.E. ("Before the Common Era") and C.E. ("Common Era") were introduced to create a more universal framework that could be utilized by people of all faiths. This shift, along with the near-universal adoption of the Gregorian calendar for civil purposes—irrespective of the religious identities of most users—challenges Rabbi Hutner's assertion that the calendar retains an explicitly Christian character.

Hutner further argues that celebrating Gentile holidays is obviously wrong. Rabbi Hutner concludes:

> "The reality of the matter is, it is necessary to distance yourself from these [idolatrous] customs and [customs that resemble them] … The truth [of the prohibition] is [nevertheless] simple and obvious."[68]

An analogous approach, albeit less certain of a prohibition, is adopted by Rabbi Menashe Klein who also rules that halacha prohibits the celebration of Thanksgiving.[69] Rabbi Klein notes that halacha divides Gentile rituals into two distinct categories. In the first category are those things that Gentiles do out of silliness and irrationality. In the second are those that are done for religious purposes or for purposes of immodesty. Rabbi Klein then cites Gra, who rules that all Gentile customs and laws that don't have Jewish origins should be avoided because they might have origins in the idolatrous customs of the past.[70] Rabbi Klein then states:

> "…[regarding] those who eat Turkey [on Thanksgiving], I heard that this is because [for the historical Pilgrims] there was nothing for them to eat, and they found this bird and rejoiced and gave thanks on [its discovery]. Therefore, [since there is a reason for eating Turkey on Thanksgiving], it would not be included in the prohibition of 'the ways of the Emorites'.
>
> However, this practice needs further investigation, as it is [still] connected to their [Gentile] holiday. See [Shulchan Aruch] YD 148:7 which states that "if a Gentile makes

---

[68] A similar type of argument can be found, relating to a different holiday, in *Kovetz Igrot Me'et HaChazon Ish*, 97.

[69] *Mishneh Halachot* 10:116. This teshuva is found in Appendix VIII within the letter of Rabbi Yehuda Henkin.

[70] Gra, *YD* 178:7.

a personal festival, [which will include] praising their deities, [such as] on their birthday or on the day that they shave their beard, and so forth" [it is prohibited to do business with them that day]; this prohibition could perhaps apply to [Thanksgiving where] Gentiles praise [their deity] [for] the discovery of this bird. They claim to thank God, blessed be He, rather than idols for finding this bird, but in [their concept of monotheism] there is [the trinitarian concept of God], God forbid that I know [of such concepts]."[71] If [they are praising a trinitarian concept of God], then it would be included in [the prohibited category] of Gentile holidays [because] they [praise a non-monotheistic God] in the ways of their ancestors. [Given these concerns], certainly this holiday

---

[71] Rabbi J. David Bleich offered a compelling response to this perspective, stating (in an email to the author) that:

> "Thanksgiving was a seudat hodaah (feast of gratitude) established by Puritans—strict monotheists who came to America precisely because they were persecuted for their opposition to avodah zarah (idolatry). What's the problem?"

This observation is significant. It is important to clarify, however, that the Thanksgiving Pilgrims were not technically Puritans. While Puritans sought to reform the Church of England from within, the Pilgrims were "Separatists" who left the Church entirely to avoid persecution. Despite this political distinction, both groups shared a core commitment to strict monotheistic beliefs. Far from being idol worshipers, the Pilgrims adhered to a unitarian concept of God and sought refuge in America to practice their faith freely. Although Thanksgiving has evolved over time, its origins remain firmly rooted in non-idolatrous principles, emphasizing gratitude and religious freedom. Rabbi Bleich further argued that even if one were to find themselves in a society where Thanksgiving had acquired pagan associations, this would not affect its permissibility within a monotheistic framework. He noted that just as the Jewish celebration of Shavuot would not be invalidated if pagans adopted it, the foundational meaning of Thanksgiving remains untainted for monotheists, as its origins are free from pagan influence.

is not appropriate for Jews to join [festively] with the Gentiles, God forbid, and the Rabbis would not approve [of one who does so]. Perhaps there is [even this] biblical prohibition [of celebrating Gentile holidays]...[72]

Rabbi Klein thus strongly discourages and perhaps even forbids the celebration of Thanksgiving.[73]

In response to this perspective, Rabbi J. David Bleich's remarks (see note 71) is important. 'Thanksgiving was a *seudat hodaah* (feast of gratitude) established by Puritans, who were strict monotheists and came to America to escape persecution for their opposition to *avodah zarah* (idolatry). What's the problem?' This insight is particularly significant. Historically, the Pilgrims were not idol worshipers; they upheld a unitarian view of God and sought freedom in America to practice their

---

[72] Rabbi Klein concludes by asserting that while the practice of eating a Thanksgiving turkey meal has a valid rationale—thereby avoiding the prohibition against imitating Gentile customs—there may still be a separate prohibition against celebrating Gentile holidays. This concern is particularly heightened due to the problematic Trinitarian concept of God associated with Christian theology. Consequently, he advises against such practices, especially given the possibility of a biblical prohibition (Mishneh Halachot 10:116, reproduced in Appendix X). The first prohibition, concerning imitation of Gentile customs, is addressed in Shulchan Aruch, Yoreh De'ah 178, while the second, regarding participation in Gentile holidays, is discussed in Yoreh De'ah 148. Although both issues pertain to interactions with non-Jewish culture, they are conceptually distinct and unrelated.

[73] Rabbi Menashe Klein, in a letter to Rabbi Ephraim Greenblatt who posed the question, states that he would withdraw his response if Rabbi Moshe Feinstein's opinion on the matter were known (*Mishneh Halachot* 10:116, also reproduced in Appendix X). Rabbi Yehuda Henkin, in a letter to this author, appears to indicate that Rabbi Klein did indeed retract his ruling out of deference to Rabbi Feinstein (see Appendix VIII). However, Rabbi Klein's expression of deference in his letter to Rabbi Greenblatt could also be interpreted as a humble colloquialism, reflecting his reverence for Rabbi Feinstein as a Torah giant rather than an actual retraction of his position. Consequently, it remains uncertain to what extent Rabbi Feinstein's view, discussed earlier, might influence or override Rabbi Klein's ruling.

beliefs without interference. While the theme of Thanksgiving as a celebration of religious freedom has evolved over time, its origins remain rooted in the values of Christian monotheists, not in paganism.

Rabbi Bleich further argues that even if one found themselves in a society where Thanksgiving was celebrated in a pagan fashion, the holiday's original, non-pagan roots would permit monotheists to observe it meaningfully. He likens this to the hypothetical scenario in which a pagan culture adopts the Jewish holiday of Shavuot; this would not hinder Jewish observance of Shavuot in its true, original sense.[74]

In contrast, Rabbi David Cohen (of Congregation Gvul Yavetz in Brooklyn) takes a stricter stance on Thanksgiving celebrations. He writes:

> "Concerning this matter [the celebration of Thanksgiving Day], there is a dispute among several Rabbinic authorities. Some prohibit [Thanksgiving observance] entirely, maintaining that it is tangential to idolatry and thus severely prohibited, while others permit it fully. In my humble opinion, consuming turkey specifically for this holiday falls under the category of prohibited Gentile customs, as referenced by Tosafot (Tractate Avodah Zarah 11a), which considers this a nonsensical and meaningless practice of theirs. Following the Gentiles in such a practice is therefore included in this prohibition. However, there is no prohibition against a family

---

[74] For more on the Pilgrims and Puritans, see the Wikipedia entry under 'Pilgrims (Plymouth Colony)' and Johnson, Daniel L. Theology and Identity: Traditions, Movements, and Polity in the United Church of Christ. Cleveland, Ohio: United Church Press, 1990, p. 4. It is important to note that the Thanksgiving Pilgrims were not technically Puritans; while Puritans sought to reform the Church of England from within, the Pilgrims were 'Separatists' who left England to avoid persecution after breaking away from the Church entirely. Nevertheless, both groups shared a core monotheistic theology, with their differences being primarily political rather than theological.

gathering and dining together simply because it is a day off from work. If they choose to eat turkey not for the sake of Thanksgiving but because they enjoy it, there is no prohibition. Nevertheless, the Rabbis would disapprove, as it gives the appearance of following Gentile customs."[75]

---

[75] Rabbi David Cohen's letter, dated 9 Nissan 5755, is transcribed in Appendix IX. Additionally, Rabbi Feivel Cohen (author of the renowned *Badai HaShulchan* series and unrelated to Rabbi David Cohen of Gvul Yavetz) wrote an undated letter to me, received in Nissan 5755, asserting that halacha prohibits celebrating Thanksgiving. He further argued, based on Maimonides (*Laws of Kings* 10:9), that Gentile participation in Thanksgiving is problematic. In Rabbi Feivel Cohen's view, Thanksgiving constitutes a "day of rest" and a "private festival" for Gentiles—both of which Maimonides prohibits. He contended that Thanksgiving represents an effort by Gentiles to create a new day of festivity, which is therefore impermissible. Moreover, he posited that even if Thanksgiving is no different from Independence Day, both are prohibited as Gentile festivals since Maimonides explicitly forbids Gentiles from adding new festivals to the calendar. For the full text of his letter, see Appendix VII.

In my analysis, however, the claim that Maimonides prohibits Thanksgiving celebrations for Gentiles is not entirely persuasive. While Thanksgiving is a legal holiday in the United States, it is not clear whether its observance meets the halachic definition of a *mo'ed* (festival) or a true "day of rest" (*shabbat*). Thanksgiving appears more as a commemoration than a festival. Furthermore, the prohibition against a Gentile observing Shabbat or any day of rest is effectively nullified if the individual deviates in any way from traditional Jewish Shabbat observance. For instance, a Gentile who performs a simple act like turning on a light or driving a car would no longer be considered as "resting" in the halachic sense. For a detailed discussion, see Rabbi J. David Bleich, "Observance of Shabbat by Prospective Proselytes," *Tradition* 25:3 (1991): 46–62.

Similarly, one might argue that Thanksgiving observance by Gentiles—given its unique character and lack of resemblance to traditional Shabbat or holiday rituals—does not fulfill the criteria for halachic prohibition. Its status as a national commemoration focused on gratitude, rather than a religiously grounded *mo'ed* or *shabbat*, renders the application of Maimonides' ruling to this context tenuous.

This juxtaposition of views highlights the range of halachic perspectives on Thanksgiving, encompassing both permissive and restrictive stances within Jewish law.

Adding to the restrictive approach is Rabbi Avigdor Miller, who opposed any form of Thanksgiving celebration, viewing it as a fundamentally Christian holiday. In one of his Thursday night lectures,[76] he stated, 'What's my opinion of Jews eating turkey on Thanksgiving? What's my opinion of going to church on Thanksgiving? I've consulted three encyclopedias… Each one states as follows: "Thanksgiving is a church holiday." Forget about a legal holiday; forget about an American holiday—it's a church holiday, created for the purpose of attending church and holding services. … I don't ask Gedolim about Thanksgiving; I ask goyim what Thanksgiving is. And three reliable goyim wrote in encyclopedias that Thanksgiving is a church holiday. They're my poskim.'[77]

---

[76] Rabbi Avigdor Miller, Lecture #529 'The *Mitzvah* of Happiness.'

[77] Cited in "Thanksgiving: Harmless Holiday or *Chukos HaGoyim*" by Rabbi Yehuda Spitz. https://ohr.edu/6105#_edn17.
My friend, Rabbi Yona Reiss, Av Bet Din of the Chicago Rabbinical Council, recounts that: "My wife's uncle was a staunch acolyte of Rabbi Avigdor Miller, but every year he hosted a Thanksgiving dinner for the family in his apartment in Borough Park. He was partially motivated by his patriotism, but there was also another side to it. As a quadriplegic, he was not able to go to children for Yomim Tovim, and he would find occasions throughout the year – such as Purim, Chanukah, and yes, Thanksgiving – to invite the extended family to his small apartment. This is another important function of Thanksgiving in that it provides a basis for a family to come together, whether religious or secular. I suspect that many observant Jewish families who get together regularly on Shabbos, Yom Tov, and family simchos throughout the year, feel less and less a need to celebrate Thanksgiving (not necessarily based on philosophical reasons, but practical ones), especially as there seems to be less of a patriotic fervor nowadays associated with the holiday."

Despite these Rabbis opposing Thanksgiving, it is interesting to note that the annual Agudas Yisrael Convention used to take place over the Thanksgiving weekend where turkey was served.

Summation of the Approaches

In summary, three premier authorities of the previous generation have taken three conflicting views. Rabbi Hutner perceived Thanksgiving as a Gentile holiday, and thus prohibited any involvement with it. Rabbi Soloveitchik permitted the celebration of Thanksgiving and permitted eating turkey on that day. He ruled that Thanksgiving was not a religious holiday and saw no problem with its celebration. Rabbi Feinstein adopted a middle ground. He maintained that Thanksgiving was not a religious holiday but that there were problems associated with "celebrating" any secular holiday. Thus, while he appears to have permitted eating turkey on that day as a festive meal, he would discourage any fixed annual "celebration."[78]

---

[78] The permissibility of observing or attending a Thanksgiving Day parade depends on the halachic classification of the day itself. Applying the three positions discussed earlier to the specific issue of parades leads to the following conclusions:

- **Thanksgiving as a Gentile Holiday:** If Thanksgiving is considered a Gentile holiday, it would be prohibited to watch, participate in, or derive any significant benefit from a parade honoring the day.
- **Thanksgiving as a Prohibited Gentile Custom:** If Thanksgiving is not deemed a Gentile holiday but is still prohibited due to the general prohibition against observing Gentile customs, watching a Thanksgiving parade would not itself be prohibited, as parades are not inherently irrational. However, caution would still be advised to avoid further entanglement with Gentile customs. (See the letter of Rabbi David Cohen, dated 9 Nissan 5755, in Appendix IX.)
- **Thanksgiving as a Secular Holiday:** If Thanksgiving is classified as a secular holiday grounded in a rational appreciation of national gratitude, watching a Thanksgiving parade would likely be permissible, comparable to attending an Independence Day parade.

V. Further Issue Related to Celebrating Thanksgiving

The issue of adding a day of celebration to the Jewish calendar is something discussed by both Rabbis Feinstein and Hutner and deserves elaboration. Rabbi Hutner asserts that the dating of such a holiday through the Christian calendar is clear evidence that such a holiday is inherently "Gentile" in nature and therefore prohibited.[79] Rabbi Feinstein

> However, specific concerns arise regarding attendance at the official Macy's Thanksgiving Day Parade. Originating in 1924 as a Christmas Parade to mark the start of the holiday shopping season, it was rebranded as a Thanksgiving parade in 1927, with the addition of balloon floats. Despite its evolution into a celebration of pop culture, the parade still features Santa Claus as its final float, symbolizing the start of the Christmas shopping season. This connection to Christmas may raise questions about participation in or endorsement of the parade. For further details on the parade's history, see Robert M. Grippo and Christopher Hoskins, Macy's Thanksgiving Day Parade (Charlotte, NC: Arcadia Publishing, 2004).
>
> Although the Macy's Thanksgiving Day Parade historically originated as a Christmas celebration, it has undeniably evolved into a primarily secular cultural event, with its religious associations largely fading into obscurity. Even the inclusion of Santa Claus, once emblematic of the parade's Christmas roots, now serves predominantly as a symbol of consumer culture and the commercial holiday season, devoid of significant religious connotation. Therefore, the three conclusions outlined above can be reasonably extended to this parade as well.

[79] Rabbi Hutner's argument, in my view, is open to challenge. According to his reasoning, it would follow that Independence Day, Labor Day, V-E Day, President's Day, and numerous other distinctly secular holidays observed by Americans throughout the year—each tied to the Christian/secular calendar—should also be classified as "Gentile" holidays. This conclusion seems counterintuitive, as the so-called "Gentile calendar" is simultaneously the secular civil calendar universally employed in America. Furthermore, Thanksgiving appears to be an especially weak example of the issue Rabbi Hutner critiques. Unlike many holidays fixed to specific dates on the calendar, Thanksgiving is not tied to a particular date but rather falls

understands this problem differently. Rabbi Feinstein maintains that there are specific halachic problems associated with adding holidays to the Jewish calendar, independent of whether they are "secular," "Jewish," or "Gentile." Indeed, these various types of objections have been raised to the modern observances of Yom HaShoah, Yom Ha'Atzma'ut, and Yom Yerushalayim, and have nothing to do with any possible Gentile origin. There is extensive literature on this issue, with many different opinions advanced.

Some authorities maintain, as Rabbi Feinstein appears to do,[80] that it is absolutely prohibited to add holidays to the calendar as annual observances.[81] These authorities rule that while individuals may celebrate such events on the anniversary of the day that they happened, these celebrations must never become incorporated into the general Jewish calendar, because it is prohibited to do so. Others maintain that such events may only be incorporated into the calendar after they receive unanimous (perhaps multi-generational) rabbinic sanction.[82] Yet others rule that any Jewish community can incorporate days of thanksgiving (or mourning) to reflect significant manifestations of God's will toward

---

on the fourth Thursday of November, irrespective of the exact date. In principle, Congress could change the date entirely—moving it, for instance, to July—without altering its essential character. This flexibility highlights Thanksgiving's detachment from rigid calendrical or religious frameworks, further undermining the claim that it embodies the concerns Rabbi Hutner raises.

[80] While Rabbi Feinstein explicitly identifies this concern, he also acknowledges in his teshuva to his grandson, Rabbi Tendler (*Igrot Moshe*, YD 4:12), that the issue of adding extra days of celebration to the Jewish calendar warrants further study. He suggests that there may be exceptions to this prohibition, leaving room for nuance in its application. For a more detailed discussion, see the conclusion of Appendix XI.

[81] This is explicitly stated by Rabbi Hutner, as noted above, and is similarly addressed by Rabbi Moshe Shternbuch in *Teshuvot v'Hanhagot* 2:721.

[82] See, for example, *Kovetz Igrot me-et HaChazon Ish* 97.

their community.[83] Some limit this to rituals that require no specialized blessings or ceremonies.[84] No consensus has emerged on this issue, and each community follows its own custom and rulings.[85]

However, in this author's opinion, a strong case can be made that this dispute is not applicable to the way Thanksgiving is, in fact, celebrated in America. Furthermore, even those who flatly prohibit any addition to the Jewish calendar are not referring to the festivities of American Independence Day, Thanksgiving, or Labor Day. Rather, these authorities are referring to the highly ritualized religious expressions of thanks to God that accompany days of religious observance, such as the services on Yom Ha'Atzma'ut and the like. Thanksgiving, like Independence Day and Labor Day, lacks any centralized prayer component, obligatory liturgy, or the requirement of a religous festival (mo'ed).[86] Even the holiday meal that many eat is not obligatory under American law.[87] Given the

---

[83] Rabbi Herzog discusses this issue in *Pesakim u'Ketavim Shel Harav Herzog*, vol. 2, OC 99–100 and 104, while Rabbi Unterman addresses it in *Shevet mi'Yehuda* 2:58. Rabbi Feinstein also explores this possibility in *Igrot Moshe*, YD 4:12; for further details, see Appendix XI.

[84] For an example of this, see Rabbi Ovadia Yosef, *Yabia Omer* OC 6:41-42.

[85] For a review essay on these various issues see, Rabbi Moshe Tzvi Neriah, "Adding Days of Joy to the Jewish Calendar," *HaTorah v'HaMedina*, vol. 3 (2nd ed. Tzomet, 5752), 77-85.

[86] It is important to recognize that this was not always the case in the United States. In the early 1950s, amidst concerns about the perceived threat of "godless communism," efforts were made to ritualize the celebration of various American holidays. "Prayer books" containing rituals and pseudo-religious "reflections" were published to promote this practice. A notable example is Mordecai Kaplan, Paul Williams, and Eugene Kohn's *The Faith of America: Prayers, Readings, and Songs for the Celebration of American Holidays* (New York, 1951). However, as far as this author observes, such rituals have completely disappeared from contemporary practice.

[87] Nor, for that matter, are the Independence Day cookout or the Veteran's Day parade considered religious or ritualistic in nature.

Michael J. Broyde

way that the completely secular[88] holidays are celebrated nowadays in America, one would not think that any of them, including Thanksgiving, is an additional "festival" in the Jewish calendar.[89] Under this approach, Rabbi Feinstein's caveat might only limit the ritualized celebration of Thanksgiving.[90] Indeed, it is precisely this type of "celebration" that

[88] In addition to Thanksgiving, the United States observes a range of national holidays that reflect the key milestones and values that have shaped the nation's identity. Martin Luther King Jr. Day honors the enduring legacy of the civil rights leader who fought for justice and equality. President's Day celebrates the birthdays of George Washington and Abraham Lincoln, two leaders who profoundly influenced the country's foundation and principles. Memorial Day solemnly honors those who sacrificed their lives in service to the nation, while Independence Day commemorates the signing of the Declaration of Independence, symbolizing the country's fight for freedom. Labor Day recognizes the contributions of workers and the labor movement in securing essential rights and protections. Columbus Day marks Christopher Columbus's arrival in the Americas, while Veterans Day pays tribute to all military service members for their dedication and sacrifices. Juneteenth celebrates the end of slavery, a pivotal moment in the nation's pursuit of justice and equality. Together, these holidays represent the diverse and significant moments that define American history and values.

[89] In this critical respect, American holidays stand in stark contrast to their Israeli counterparts, whose ritualized practices often bear the hallmarks of additions to the Jewish calendar. While the establishment of the State of Israel and the halachic responses it evokes are profoundly significant topics, this book does not seek to provide an exhaustive analysis of those issues. Rather, the focus of this section is to underscore that such considerations are not pertinent to the halachic discussions surrounding the observance of modern American secular holidays.

[90] Consistent with this approach is Rabbi Henkin's proposal (discussed in the previous section) to skip the Thanksgiving meal every few years as a means of demonstrating that it is not a religious ritual. He similarly understands Rabbi Feinstein's concerns as being focused on the potential for ritualization. As a practical example of not always adhering to Thanksgiving traditions, one of my children was married on Thanksgiving Day, underscoring the flexibility and non-religious nature of the holiday.

Rabbi Feinstein frowns upon and with which Rabbi Henkin concedes to him on.⁹¹

One additional point merits attention: all three authorities seem to concur that celebrating a one-time day of thanksgiving to commemorate a significant event worthy of gratitude is not halachically problematic.⁹²

---

⁹¹ See Appendix VIII for Rabbi Henkin's discussion of Rabbi Feinstein's guidance on Thanksgiving, emphasizing that it should not be treated as an obligatory observance. Rabbi Henkin interprets Rabbi Feinstein's position as advising against a ritualized celebration, while permitting an annual meal if approached as an optional custom. In line with this interpretation, Rabbi Henkin suggests skipping the Thanksgiving meal every few years to reinforce its non-obligatory nature.

In my view, changes in American society and culture since the 1950s may help explain the differences between Rabbi Feinstein's initial responsum in 1953 and his final one in 1980. When Rabbi Feinstein first addressed this issue, Thanksgiving was widely recognized as a secular holiday, but some voices were advocating for its religious institutionalization (see note 84 for more details). At the time, Rabbi Feinstein recommended that *baalei nefesh* (pious individuals) adopt a stringent stance due to these potential religious connotations. By 1980, however, such efforts had largely dissipated from American culture, and Thanksgiving had become firmly established as a secular celebration. This cultural shift likely influenced Rabbi Feinstein's more lenient stance in his final *teshuva* (*Igrot Moshe*, YD 4:12), where he focuses on Thanksgiving's merits purely as a secular observance.

However, in *Igrot Moshe*, OC 5:20:6, also written in 1980, Rabbi Feinstein references his 1953 ruling for *baalei nefesh*, suggesting that some caution may still be warranted, which complicates a straightforward interpretation. For a more comprehensive analysis of Rabbi Feinstein's evolving positions, see Appendix XI.

⁹² Although it is not clear that Rabbi Hutner would agree, a close reading of his letter does seem to imply it, since the basis for his prohibition of Thanksgiving is it being a fixed holiday on the Gentile calendar. Indeed, Rabbi Hutner states in *Pachad Yitzchak* 109:

> "About your question [regarding celebrating Thanksgiving], if this is a biblical or rabbinic [violation], behold this entire investigation would not have been [important] if it was judged [to be] in the category of a one-time festival."

See Appendix VI for a translation of the rest of this section of *Pachad Yitzchak*.

For example, President Bush's 1991 declaration of a day of thanksgiving following the victory in the Persian Gulf War[93] would not raise any issues, including the permissibility of holding celebratory events. In fact, as Rabbi Feinstein notes, there is precedent for such expressions of thanksgiving in Talmudic tradition, further supporting the permissibility of this type of observance.[94]

VI. Conclusion:

Three key conclusions from this book warrant attention:

First, contemporary authorities present three primary approaches to the question of celebrating Thanksgiving. Some poskim rule that Thanksgiving is not a Gentile holiday but nonetheless place limits on its "celebration." Others categorically prohibit any involvement, as they view it as a Gentile holiday. A third group permits full participation in Thanksgiving observances, considering it a secular holiday and even deeming such celebrations wise and proper when they promote patriotism and other positive American values.

This diversity reflects an ongoing fundamental debate among American halachic authorities over the past one hundred years. The central issue lies in whether halacha should distinguish between "secular society," "religious-Gentile society," and "idol-worshiping society" in the context of modern American culture. These distinctions, though without clear precedent, have significant implications for a wide range of halachic questions related to life in contemporary America. As with many areas of halacha where diverse approaches exist, individuals should adhere

---

[93] For a discussion on this, see *California School Employees Association v. Governing Board of the Marin Community College District*, 33 Cal.Rptr.2d 109 (1994).

[94] See *Igrot Moshe YD* 4:11:4 which cites, in *Kiddushin* 66a, that King Yannai held a celebration in honor of his conquest of *Kochalit* in the desert and that the Sages attended such a celebration.

to the guidance of their community, family, or rabbi, while respecting and accepting as legitimate the differing practices of others. This respect for diverse halachic interpretations, sanctioned by rabbinic authority, fosters unity among observant Jews—a unity for which we can offer true thanksgiving to the Almighty.

Second, this book has intentionally avoided prescribing normative halachic rulings, focusing instead on the broader issues. However, some conclusions are unavoidable. In this author's view, the analysis establishes the following:

1. Thanksgiving is a secular holiday with secular origins.
2. While some individuals celebrate Thanksgiving with religious rituals, the vast majority of Americans do not.[95]
3. Halacha permits celebrating secular holidays, provided one avoids participating in observances that involve religious worship.[96]
4. It is essential to prevent Thanksgiving from taking on the appearance of a religious obligation. This can be achieved, for example, by occasionally forgoing the Thanksgiving meal, signaling that it is not treated as a religious duty. This final point aligns with Rabbi Feinstein's concerns.

As such, I feel that halacha permits one to have a private Thanksgiving celebration with one's Jewish or secular friends and family; for many in our American community, Thanksgiving meals provide a valuable moment to unite with one's family while avoiding the many complexities of Shabbat and Yom Tov with non-halachically observant family. Furthermore, as loyal citizens and given the gratitude we feel towards the United States government, I would even suggest that such conduct is wise and proper, particularly in current times when antisemitism is

---

[95] As stated by Rabbi Henkin in the discussion above, Letter of Rabbi Henkin dated 23 *Tevet* 5755 published in *Bnei Banim* 3:37, also found in Appendix VIII.

[96] Ibid.

on the rise. We ought to role model patriotism and loyalty, even if these values are not always part of the modern American Thanksgiving. As noted above, Thanksgiving was marked to some extent by Rabbi Joseph B. Soloveitchik, thus adding weight to the legitimacy of marking the day in some manner

Finally, an important reflection: Rabbi Joseph B. Soloveitchik offers a model for integrating Torah values into Thanksgiving observance. On Thanksgiving Day, he would adjust the timing of his shiur—beginning and ending earlier—to allow time to celebrate with his family. Crucially, he did not reduce the time devoted to Torah study or cancel the shiur. Instead, he restructured the day to balance his commitment to Torah learning with participation in the day's civic festivities. This thoughtful approach provides a valuable framework for how we might observe Thanksgiving: engaging in the day's celebrations while maintaining Torah study as a cornerstone of our lives.

Rabbi Soloveitchik's practice reminds us that Torah learning is not a duty to be sidelined but a continuous and integral part of a meaningful life, even on days that invite other priorities. Following his example, communities might consider arranging a dedicated shiur after davening on Thanksgiving morning, creating an opportunity for shared learning that reflects our values. This integration ensures that Torah study remains central to our observance of Thanksgiving, enriching both our gratitude and our commitment to a life of learning.

Introduction To Appendices I-III

This book proposes a conceptual Punnett square to categorize American federal holidays according to halacha. The first square represents holidays with secular origins that are celebrated purely in a secular manner, such as Columbus Day, Veterans Day, and Thanksgiving.[1] In the diagonally opposite square are holidays with religious origins that are still observed with religious significance by many, such as Christmas.[2] Adjacent to this is the square for holidays of religious origin that are now celebrated in a secular fashion. While these holidays have undisputed religious origins, they no longer carry religious significance in their contemporary celebrations. Examples include Halloween, Valentine's Day, and New Year's Day. Diagonally opposite this square are holidays with secular origins that have come to be observed with religious or nationalistic overtones. Examples might include the coronation of a new king or queen in England[3] or certain

---

[1] Rabbi Hutner advanced the novel idea that even these types of secular holidays celebrated at a specific date on the Christian calendar are to be considered Christian, rather than secular. Most *halachic* authorities are not deeply impressed with this argument because the Christian calendar itself has become secular and not Christian.

[2] So would celebrating St. Patrick's Day, which is not a federal holiday in America but is in Ireland.

[3] Indeed, while the modern coronation of a monarch in England does involve many different faiths in attendance, it is still based on explicit Church of England doctrines. Taking place in Westminster Abbey church, and officiated by its Archbishop of Canterbury, the monarch explicitly declares to uphold its doctrines and beliefs. See: https://www.royal.uk/the-coronation-history-and-ceremonial

According to the above, it would seem that one could even claim it is forbidden for any Jew to watch this coronation ceremony's live broadcast in any capacity. See https://www.torahweb.org/torah/special/2005/papalFuneral.html where Rabbi Soloveitchik's students prohibited watching Pope John Paul II's funeral on TV, based on Rabbi Soloveitchik not allowing the watching of President

Shinto-influenced national holidays in Japan.[4]

Secular Origins and Secular Celebrations Today: Columbus Day, Veterans Day and Thanksgiving	Secular Origins and Religious Celebrations Today: None in America now
Religious Origins, but Fully Secular Celebrations Today: Halloween, Valentine's Day and New Year's Day	Religious Origins and Religious Celebrations Today: Christmas

This book has already examined Thanksgiving in depth, exploring the varied approaches of different poskim. In the following three appendices, we turn to several American holidays that, though rooted in religious origins, are now celebrated in a secular manner.

Kennedy's funeral since it took place as a Catholic Mass. For why government Rabbis and other officials do seem to be permitted to attend a church ceremony such as a coronation, see "Entering a Sanctuary for Hatzalat Yisrael: An Exchange" By: Michael J. Broyde and Kenneth Auman **https://hakirah.org/Vol%208%20 Broyde.pdf**. In truth, I wonder if the Rav's ruling regarding television in 1963 still reflects a correct understanding of what 'participating' in a church ceremony means. Maybe this prohibition is now limited to Zoom and not YouTube. More information is needed.

4 After WWII, the United States demanded that Japan separate the Shinto religion from the national government due to their belief that it had been responsible for Japan's militarism and nationalism. One of the consequences of "The Shinto Directive" was the creation of new "national, secular holidays" such as "Vernal Equinox Day" which replaced Shinto festivals. However, despite these being secular holidays, most of Japan observe them based on the older Shinto festivals. For more see: https://www.bbc.co.uk/religion/religions/shinto/history/nationalism_1.shtml

Appendix I

Halloween Trick or Treating

As we have seen, the prevailing view among the poskim is that marking Thanksgiving with a turkey meal is permitted according to halacha and, as Rabbi Belsky observed, may even be encouraged when it serves as an expression of patriotism. This perspective is supported by the conclusion, upheld by many halachic authorities, that:

1. Thanksgiving is a secular holiday with secular origins.

2. While some people celebrate Thanksgiving with religious rituals, this is unusual, and, therefore, does not cause Thanksgiving to be classified as a Christian holiday.

3. *Halakha* permits one to celebrate secular holidays though one must not do so with people who religiously celebrate them.

As a result, most *poskim*, including Rabbis Feinstein, and Soloveitchik, permit one to have a private Thanksgiving celebration with one's Jewish or secular friends and family, so long as one does not treat Thanksgiving as a religious ritual or holiday.[1] Such conduct is proper in my view, and I generally celebrate Thanksgiving. However, to comply with the view of Rabbi Yehuda Henkin, I celebrate Thanksgiving without any religious fervor, and I occasionally skip a year.[2]

Shortly after my views on Thanksgiving first appeared, I was asked about the permissibility of "trick or treating" on Halloween. I concluded that *halacha* prohibits celebrating Halloween with the wearing of a

---

[1] See Chapter IV.

[2] This was the case a few years ago when my eldest son was married to the lovely Suzanne [nee Bodian] Broyde on Thanksgiving Day. See also the dedication to the book.

costume and going door to door collecting candy. This is due to the fact that Halloween has clear pagan origins. As per History.com:

> The tradition originated with the ancient Celtic festival of *Samhain*, when people would light bonfires and wear costumes to ward off ghosts. In the eighth century, Pope Gregory III designated November 1 as a time to honor all saints. Soon, All Saints Day incorporated some of the traditions of *Samhain*. The evening before was known as All Hallows Eve, and later Halloween. Over time, Halloween evolved into a day of activities like trick-or-treating, carving jack-o-lanterns, festive gatherings, donning costumes and eating treats.[3]

On another History.com webpage we read:

> The importance of pre-Christian customs to people's lives apparently wasn't lost upon the early Catholic Church. Pope Gregory I, also known as St. Gregory the Great, who headed the Church from A.D. 590 to 604, advised a missionary going to England that instead of trying to do away with the religious customs of non-Christian peoples, they simply should convert them to a Christian religious purpose. For example, "the site of a pagan temple could be converted to become a Christian church…" In that fashion, *Samhain*, the Celts' dark supernatural festival, eventually was converted and given a Christian context.
>
> The ancient Celts believed that all sorts of threatening spirits were out and about on *Samhain*… The early medieval Christian church believed in saints—Christians who were remarkable for their devout religious beliefs

---

[3] See: https://www.history.com/topics/halloween/history-of-halloween.

and lives…But saints also had a supernatural side, such as their involvement in miraculous occurrences.

So the Church mixed the traditions involving Celtic spirits and Catholic saints. In the 800s, the Church designated November 1 as All Saints' Day.

> "The old beliefs associated with *Samhain* never died out entirely," folklorist Jack Santino wrote in a 1982 article for the American Folklife Center. "The powerful symbolism of the traveling dead was too strong, and perhaps too basic to the human psyche, to be satisfied with the new, more abstract Catholic feast honoring saints."
>
> Instead, the first night of *Samhain*, October 31, became All Hallows Day Evening, the night before the saints were venerated. That name eventually morphed into Halloween, and it became the time when Christians could turn the supernatural symbolism and rituals of *Samhain* into spooky fun.[4]

As such, in order to permit celebrating a holiday with clearly pagan origins, one of four conditions must be met:[5]

1. The holiday has an additional secular origin.
2. The conduct of those who celebrate the holiday can be rationally explained independent of its pagan origins.
3. The pagan origins of the holiday, or the Catholic response to it, are so deeply hidden that they have essentially been forgotten,

---

[4] https://www.history.com/news/halloween-samhain-celts-catholic-church.

[5] The source for these four basic principles is found in Rema YD 178:1, and the commentaries there.

and the celebrations can be attributed to some secular source or reason.

4. The activities and events commemorated by the holiday are consistent with Jewish tradition.

Since it was clear to me that none of these statements were true, I concluded that celebrating Halloween in any way, such as by dressing in a costume, is forbidden.[6]

A Reexamination

Yet a reconsideration is needed in light of modern times.[7] Indeed, notwithstanding the origins of Halloween, one must recognize that the vast overwhelming majority of the people in America who currently celebrate Halloween do not do so out of any sense of religious observance or feeling. Indeed, one is hard pressed to find a religion in the United States that recognizes Halloween as a religious holiday. In 1995, in response to Christian assertions that Halloween celebrations are a form of pagan worship, Cheryl S. Clark wrote as follows:

> One of my fondest memories of kindergarten was the first Halloween celebrated at school. I marched proudly from room to room in our elementary school in my Wilma Flintstone costume as a participant in the Halloween parade. The anticipation of the event was overwhelming, exciting and the fun was anything but sinister.... To say that participating in Halloween leads to devil worship is like saying taking Tylenol leads to crack addiction. Believe me, when I was marching in my Wilma Flintstone costume, the last thing on my mind was drawing pentagrams or performing satanic rituals. The

---

[6] See "Celebrating Secular Holidays," Emunah Magazine 28-32 (Fall, 2000).

[7] Indeed, I originally wrote about Halloween in 1997, which was nearly 30 years ago now.

only thought I had was that next year I'd be Pebbles!... It is only a few fringe group fundamentalists who seriously believe Halloween is a holiday for worshiping the devil.[8]

This statement appears to be a truthful recounting of the modern American celebration of Halloween. The vast majority of people who celebrate Halloween have absolutely no religious motives at all -- it is simply an excuse to collect candy, or engage in mischievous behavior, or to simply have a party.[9]

However, despite this, the simple fact is that the origins of Halloween are pagan. And yet, it is clear to anyone who lives in the real world that this letter writer from 1995 is correct and that this view has only grown more correct with the passage of time. It is obvious that today there is little religious, magical, mystical, or even Catholic aspects to Halloween. From *Sabrina the Teenage Witch* to *Buffy the Vampire Slayer* to so much more, it is apparent that we are living in the era of the witch as entertainment, and not as a religious figurehead. One needs to search hard to find Americans who celebrate Halloween religiously or are even aware of its religious origins.

Even the era of ghost and goblin costumes, representing superstition and supplication, has been replaced by the era of Wilma and Pebbles, or Barack and Donald costumes. The leading Halloween 2023 costume, found in Google's excellent Halloween web page,[10] is Barbie, followed by (2) Princess (3) Spider-Man (4) Witch (5) Fairy (6) Wednesday Addams (7) Dinosaur (8) Cowboy (9) Ninja and (10) Bunny. It is clearer now,

[8] Cheryl S. Clark, Halloween Atlanta Constitution, October 22, B1 (1995) available at https://www.newspapers.com/newspage/402908529/

[9] However, it is worth noting that there are still some people who celebrate Halloween religiously, and there are occasional court cases about employees who seek to take leave on Halloween day by claiming it as a religious holiday. See for example, Van-Koten v. Family Health Management Corporation, 955 F. Supp. 898 (N.D. Ill., 1997) as well as the more than 50 cases that refer to it or discuss it.

[10] https://frightgeist.withgoogle.com/

more than any time before, that the pagan origins of Halloween and the Catholic response to it are so deeply hidden that they have virtually disappeared. Halloween celebrations today can be attributed to a general secular culture that focuses on the fantasies of life rather than matters of faith. Of course, a witch costume can still be a religious figure placed in the same category as Mohammed or Moses, rather than being placed in the same group as Spiderman, a dinosaur, and a ninja. However, it is clear to me that in the year 2024, witches are in the second category and not the first for almost all Americans. Therefore, it emerges that a more modern and accurate identification of the contemporary American celebration of Halloween is that it has no real religious context.[11]

[11] Of course, cultural variation plays a significant role here, with the more secular regions of the United States largely removing the religious aspects of Halloween. For example, during my time as a visiting professor at Stanford University in 2019, I observed that Halloween was celebrated solely in a secular manner in Palo Alto. This shift reflects broader sociological trends. Consider the figure of Hercules: in ancient Greek and Roman mythology, he was revered as a near-divine hero, even worshipped by the faithful. In modern culture, however, Hercules is more likely to appear as a cartoon character in a Disney movie or as a supporting figure in Xena: Warrior Princess. A useful mental exercise to illustrate this transition is to consider whether Hercules belongs with figures like Moses and Mohammed or with superheroes like Batman and Spiderman. From the latter half of the 20th century onward, he is clearly grouped with the latter. Accordingly, when asked, I have permitted children to dress as Hercules on Purim (similar to Spiderman and Batman) in communities where superhero costumes are popular. We are witnessing a similar transformation with Santa Claus, who is increasingly portrayed as a secular, cartoon-like character. For instance, in the 2006 episode "Mickey Saves Santa" from Mickey Mouse Clubhouse (Season 1, Episode 20), Santa is presented without religious connotations. A quick Google search reveals numerous appearances by Santa in Disney media, while other religious figures from active faith traditions are absent. This trend suggests an evolving separation between Santa and his Christian origins, with Santa becoming a more secular figure. For further discussion, see "Santa is Welcome, but Be Careful About Religious Displays" at https://firstamendmentmuseum.org/santa-is-welcome-but-be-careful-about-religious-displays/.

Thus, the question regarding Halloween is whether *halacha* would allow one to celebrate an event or "holiday" that has pagan origins when the vast majority of people who celebrate it are now unaware and uninterested in its pagan origins. Nevertheless, since a minority of people still acknowledge and celebrate its pagan origins, it appears to me that this would still render "trick or treating" in a witch or ghost costume forbidden. Secular holidays are *halachically* complex, and Halloween is a wonderful example of the changing culture behind holidays in America and its impact on *halacha*.

Halachic Conclusions

Based on the above; in order to permit collecting candy on Halloween, one would have to accept any of the following assertions to be true:[12]

1. Halloween celebrations have a secular origin.
2. The conduct of the individuals celebrating Halloween can be rationally explained.
3. The pagan origins of Halloween, or the Catholic response to it, are so deeply hidden that they have disappeared, and the celebrations can be attributed to some secular source or reason.

---

[12] Even if Halloween celebrations today were deemed halachically permissible, a deeper philosophical (hashkafic) question remains: Should we encourage participation in celebrations that lack meaningful values simply because they contain no explicit violation? Perhaps Tosafot's concerns about foolish, secular practices should still make us wary of promoting activities like dressing up in fictional costumes and roaming the streets for candy. We must consider what meaningful values, if any, these practices impart to our children. Indeed, Rabbi David Cohen, in a letter to this author on the subject of watching the Thanksgiving Day Parade, suggests that while adults may view the parade under certain conditions, children should refrain from doing so, as it may impart improper values about celebrating the day alongside non-Jews. For his full statement, see Appendix VIII.

4. The activities and practices of Halloween are consistent with the Jewish tradition.

From the preceding discussion, it is reasonable to insist that none of these statements are true although I am not absolutely certain. The origins of Halloween are not secular in origin and the way people celebrate Halloween can be clearly connected to the Celtic/pagan origins of the holiday. Of course, there is also no Jewish basis for Halloween. In the real world, I suspect that a witch costume is much more prohibited as a matter of *halacha* than a Donald or Barack one.

Applying these *halachic* principles to Halloween leads to the conclusion that participating in Halloween celebrations -- which consists primarily of collecting candy while wearing a ghostly costume -- is prohibited as per the ruling of Rema and commentaries cited above.

As such, one should not send one's children out to "trick or treat" on Halloween in costume, or otherwise celebrate the holiday by wearing a witch or ghost costume. These things invoke its pagan Celtic origins. Indeed, a claim could be made that such conduct is a derivative of idol worship and thus a serious violation of *halacha*.

The question of whether one may give candy to children who come to the door on Halloween is distinct from the question of participating in the holiday itself. There are significant reasons based on the halachic principles of darchei shalom (ways of peace), eivah (avoiding hostility toward Jews), and similar concerns, which may justify giving candy to non-Jewish children who might feel insulted or resentful if none is offered. This consideration is particularly relevant in neighborhoods with Jewish residents who, often without awareness of any halachic issues, actively participate in the holiday's customs, including 'trick-or-treating.' Thus, if one feels it necessary, one may give candy to children—Jewish or non-Jewish—who come to the door, prioritizing communal harmony while recognizing the distinctions in practice.

A related question is whether one must prevent one's own children from taking Halloween candy when it is offered to them in public. (For example, one goes with one's children to a store on Halloween day, and there is free *kosher* candy being given out.) It is clear in such a situation that children do not intend to celebrate anything and simply want some free candy which would make them equally happy on any day of the year. As such, it is permissible for children to accept the candy. It is probably wise to reinforce to one's children in such situations that Jews do not celebrate Halloween.[13]

Finally, a Jewish teacher in a public school that observes Halloween in a secular manner, as part of the cycle of secular school holidays, need not feel compelled to resign rather than participate in these events. Several reasons support this conclusion. First, public schools are required to celebrate events like Halloween in a purely secular way, allowing teachers to rely on the non-religious nature of these school celebrations.[14] Second, a teacher in this context educates without endorsing or promoting any specific practices. Lastly, there does not appear[15] to be an obligation for a teacher in a public school setting to prevent students from engaging in

---

[13] This is purely pedagogic and not a halachic concern, at least directly.

[14] A reviewer asked me if I would also allow a public-school teacher to participate in public school Christmas celebrations under the same rationale. The question of whether secular celebrations of religious events is permitted is clear: The answer is no. The leniency regarding Halloween is because although it has pagan origins, it is no longer celebrated religiously by nearly the entire American public. Christmas, on the other hand, is a religious holiday to many Americans. (This is the reality in most of the world. In Japan, however, it is clear that Christmas is a secular holiday. See for example https://www.jrpass.com/blog/do-people-celebrate-christmas-in-japan "Though Japan does celebrate Christmas, it does so in a distinctly different way than the American or European traditions call for. Japanese culture is shaped in many ways by the Buddhist religion, and only about 1% of the population is Christian.")

[15] Parents who send their children to such schools are 'willful', either because they think this conduct is permitted or because they do not care. In such cases a number of authorities rule that the prohibition of "assisting people to sin" does not apply when they will sin without your "assistance" anyways. For more on this, See Michael Broyde and David Hertzberg, Enabling a Jew to Sin: The Parameters in Journal of Halacha and Contemporary Society 19 (1990), 5–36.

activities that might conflict with halacha. However, it would likely be both unwise and inappropriate for a teacher in this role to wear a costume, as this may give an unintended impression of personal endorsement. Additionally, it is worth noting that New Year's Day—another holiday with religious origins that is now celebrated in a secular manner—raises similar questions. Later sections will address this comparison in more depth, considering whether New Year's observance aligns more closely with Halloween or differs in relevant respects. For now, it suffices to acknowledge that both holidays share these complex issues, though each carries distinct considerations in halacha.

Appendix II

Valentine's Day

A Brief History of Valentine's Day[1]

In Ancient Rome, a holiday of love known as *Lupercalia* was observed from February 13th–15th, paying homage to *Pan* and *Juno*, the pagan gods of love, marriage, and fertility. The festival, which also celebrated the coming of spring, included rituals to increase fertility and the pairing of couples through a lottery.

The modern Valentine's Day, however, seems to be an independent Christian invention. Nevertheless, it is more than likely that the Christian church decided to place St. Valentine's Day in the middle of February in an effort to "Christianize" the pagan celebration of *Lupercalia*. This was precisely the case with the institution of All Saints Day which attempted to "Christianize" Halloween. As we read in the prior appendix from History.com:

> "The importance of pre-Christian customs to people's lives apparently wasn't lost upon the early Catholic Church. Pope Gregory I, also known as St. Gregory the Great, who headed the Church from A.D. 590 to 604, advised a missionary going to England that instead of trying to do away with the religious customs of non-Christian peoples, they simply should convert them to a Christian religious purpose. For example, 'the site of a

---

[1] The majority of this section is based on information found in Encyclopedia Britannica on Valentine's Day, see: **Valentine's Day | Definition, History, & Traditions | Britannica**.

pagan temple could be converted to become a Christian church'."[2]

The contemporary St. Valentine's Day is designated to commemorate one or more early Christian martyrs named Valentine. The most likely Valentine "candidate" to be associated with this day is the 3rd-century saint who was imprisoned for ministering to Christians persecuted under the Roman Empire. He was put to death by Claudius II Gothicus.

According to an early Christian tradition, St. Valentine miraculously restored the sight of his jailer's blind daughter, which was likely the act that earned him the Sainthood. Later traditions connect him with a love theme, including an 18th-century legend that claims he wrote the jailer's daughter a letter signed "Your Valentine" as a farewell before his execution. This is likely the source for the practice of boys and girls asking each other "will you be my Valentine?" as a sign of affection. Another possible connection to love is the tradition that St. Valentine performed weddings for Christian soldiers who were forbidden to marry due to a war draft.

However, it was only from the 14th century onward that Valentine's Day became clearly associated with love and romance[3]—around seven hundred years after it ceased to be observed as a pagan festival of love. Since then, nearly all references to February 14th have centered on themes of love and courtship

---

[2] See https://www.history.com/news/halloween-samhain-celts-catholic-church for more on this idea (though the context here is the Christianization of Halloween).

[3] In his 14th-century poem Parlement of Foules, Chaucer describes birds choosing their mates on Valentine's Day, suggesting an early association between Valentine's Day and the theme of love.

Halachic Conclusions

In order to permit celebrating a holiday with clearly pagan or Christian origins, one of four conditions must be met:[4]

1. The holiday has an additional secular origin.
2. The conduct of those who celebrate the holiday can be rationally explained independent of its pagan origins.
3. The pagan origins of the holiday, or the Catholic response to it, are so deeply hidden that they have essentially been forgotten, and the celebrations can be attributed to some secular source or reason.
4. The activities and events commemorated by the holiday are consistent with Jewish tradition.

It is my feeling that while the modern Valentine's Day clearly has pagan and Christian origins, these origins have all but been forgotten by our secular society.[5] One could still suggest that just like the prior appendix prohibited Halloween in its current secular form, Valentine's Day should fare the same. However, celebrating Valentine's Day is quite different from celebrating Halloween, even though the latter has also lost much of its religious origins. This is because Halloween still has an irrational component to it, as the idea of celebrating it today, with scary costumes and by collecting candy, can only be justified and explained by tracing it back to its gentile origins. Valentine's Day, on the other

---

[4] The source for these four basic principles is found in Rema *YD* 178:1, and the commentaries there.

[5] I visited three stores that sell greeting cards to see how Valentine's Day is portrayed, and to my surprise, none of the many cards I reviewed mentioned the holiday's Christian origins or even referred to it as Saint Valentine's Day, despite its roots in Roman Catholic ritual. This secular presentation is also evident in the popular messages associated with Valentine's Day in general culture, which appear entirely devoid of religious overtones.

hand, is today celebrated in a manner that society considers to be very rational, namely, by sharing love, noting friendship, and (perhaps most importantly) eating chocolate; each of these values is not inherently religious and they can all be explained rationally, which fulfills one of Rema's above-mentioned criteria[6] for permitting Jews to observe customs with religious origins. Additionally, Valentine's Day's emphasis on spousal love is a Jewish value and is not foreign to the *halachic* tradition; this fulfills another criterion for permissibility. Thus, it seems clear that the celebration of Valentine's Day today should be permitted.

The Thanksgiving section earlier in this work made an observation which is important to recall at this time. Even when a holiday is completely pagan in origin, *halacha* does not necessarily forbid any form of "participation" whatsoever. For example, Rabbi Moshe Feinstein[7] is logically correct in his observation that:

> " ...that even [in a case] where something would be considered a prohibited Gentile custom, if the general populace of Gentiles do it for reasons unrelated to their religion or law, but rather, because it is pleasurable to them, then already there is no prohibition of imitating Gentile customs. So too, it is obvious that if Gentiles were to make a religious law to eat a particular item that is good to eat, *halacha* would not prohibit eating that item. So too, any item of pleasure in the world cannot be prohibited merely because Gentiles do so out of religious observance."

As such, I am of the view that eating chocolate on Valentine's Day, and even giving chocolate to others, without mentioning why one is doing so would be permitted even if one were to disagree with the analysis above and argue that Valentine's Day is still defined or celebrated

---

[6] YD 178:1.

[7] *Igrot Moshe*, YD 4:11:4.

as a Christian holiday. The same can be said for any activity which is intrinsically of value, such as a husband expressing his love for his wife or giving flowers to a beloved, each of which would be a nice gesture all year round. Indeed, those who know me well know that I frequently bring home sweets or flowers to my wife, Channah – without whom none of my accomplishments would be possible – as an expression of love and admiration, and that includes on Valentine's Day.[8]

Nevertheless, while celebrations may be permissible, I believe it is commendable to avoid overtly celebrating Valentine's Day. That said, bringing home chocolate, flowers, or even jewelry for one's wife is always a thoughtful gesture—on any day of the year, including February 14th.

---

[8] Years ago, one of my teachers observed that there is no prohibition against being especially kind to others during the days between December 25th and January 1st, even though this coincides with a common Christian custom. After all, practicing kindness is a fundamental Torah value at all times.

Appendix III

New Year's Day

The origins of January 1st as New Year's Day are cloaked in historical mystery. As Wikipedia notes:

> "In pre-Christian Rome, under the Julian calendar, the day was dedicated to Janus, god of gateways and beginnings, for whom January is also named. ... In Christendom, 1 January traditionally marks the Feast of the Circumcision of Christ ... As a date in the Christian calendar , New Year's Day liturgically marked the Feast of the Naming and Circumcision of Jesus, which is still observed as such in the Anglican Church, the Lutheran Church, the Eastern Orthodox Church, and in Traditional Catholicism by those who retain the usage of the General Roman Calendar of 1960. The mainstream Roman Catholic Church celebrates on this day the Solemnity of Mary, Mother of God."

However, what is absolutely clear, is that our modern celebration of January 1 is driven by a Papal decree. As one source notes:

> "A Pope Restored the January 1st Celebration: In 1582, after reform of the Gregorian calendar, Pope Gregory XIII re-established January 1st as New Year's Day. Although most Catholic countries adopted the Gregorian calendar almost immediately, it was only gradually adopted among Protestant countries. Countries belonging to the Eastern

Orthodox Church did not readily adopt the Gregorian calendar either."[1]

It is also quite clear, on a historical level, that Catholic Europe celebrated New Year's Day religiously for centuries both before and after this papal decree. Indeed, consider the simple remarks of Rema, writing in his *Darchei Moshe*[2] quoting the *Terumat HaDeshen*:

> "It is written in the *Terumat HaDeshen*, chapter 195, that even nowadays one who wants to send [gifts] on the eighth day after Christmas, which is called New Year's, should do so on the day before [i.e. December 31st] and not on the day of the holiday itself. However, if the day before the holiday falls out on Shabbat, then one may send gifts on the day of the holiday itself. This is because it could lead to hatred [*eiva*] if one sends gifts any later or earlier than these days."[3]

While Rema,[4] in his commentary to the *Shulchan Aruch*, does not quote this formulation exactly as it is written here, it is clear to me that this is a result of Church censorship and not because the matter is in

---

[1] https://www.ancient-origins.net/myths-legends/ancient-origins-new-years-celebrations-001181

[2] *YD* 148.

[3] There is a significant debate over whether concerns of eiva (hatred or animosity) permit only the violation of rabbinic prohibitions or extend even to biblical ones. Tosafot on Avodah Zarah 26a (s.v. savar rav yosef) suggests that eiva only justifies violating a rabbinic prohibition, not a biblical one. For further discussion, see Encyclopedia Talmudit, entry Eiva, vol. 1, p. 493. This debate, however, is not directly relevant here, as gift-giving on New Year's Day is not a religious act but a cultural custom, making it subject to, at most, rabbinic concerns. No religion mandates gift-giving on New Year's Day; it is purely a social practice.

[4] *YD* 148:12.

dispute.[5] According to Rema, New Year's Day is a Christian Holiday (indeed the formulation in the *Terumat HaDeshen* makes it clear that we are discussing the "eighth day of Christmas" as much as we are discussing New Year's Day) whose celebration must be avoided and can only be marked when long-term life-threatening hatred to our community will result if gifts are not given.

On the other hand, nowadays this reality seems to have completely changed. New Year's Day, like Valentine's Day (and in contrast to Christmas), seems to have completely lost its Christian overtone.[6] Even in the deep Christian South, where I live, there are no indicia that connect New Year's Day to Christianity. Even the "first generation" Hindu and Muslim communities in Atlanta, who would never celebrate Christmas, have New Year's Eve parties. It is obvious that the status of New Year's Day has changed in the last three hundred years.

Indeed, in contemporary America, there is little religious content or expression to New Year's Day. Few would classify it as a religious holiday, as there are clear secular practices and reasons for celebrating New Year's Day. Therefore, as per reason number 3 below, it has lost its status as a Christian holiday. Rabbi Feinstein[7] explicitly notes this himself when discussing celebrating New Year's:

> The first day of their year [January 1] ... are not prohibited according to the law, but pious people [*baalei nefesh*] should be strict [not to do so].

---

[5] Indeed, past editions of the Darchei Moshe commentary also appear to have been censored in a manner similar to the Shulchan Aruch. For the uncensored version of Darchei Moshe, see Machon Yerushalayim's edition of the Tur.

[6] This has nothing to do with the manner of celebration, which I will address in the next section. Naturally, celebrating New Year's Day through public drunkenness or by attending inappropriate gatherings violates halacha—no differently than celebrating Chanukah or even a Thursday night in such a manner.

[7] *Igrot Moshe*, EH 2:13.

This insight, written in 1953, is even more true nowadays. The Christian origins of New Year's Day are even more concealed nowadays than a half century ago.

Modes of Celebration

My own sense of the issue regarding New Year's Day, is that we must determine what we really mean by "celebrating" it. Once this question is resolved, we will have a good idea on how we should conduct ourselves from the perspective of *halacha*. Since New Year's Day clearly has pagan origins, as noted above, in order to permit participating in something that might have Christian or other religious origins, one must be able to show one of four things:[8]:

1. The holiday has an additional secular origin.
2. The conduct of the individuals celebrating the holiday can be rationally explained independent of its pagan origins.
3. The pagan origins of the holiday, or the Catholic response to it, are so deeply hidden that they have essentially been forgotten, and the celebrations can be attributed to some secular source or reason.
4. The activities and events commemorated by the holiday are consistent with Jewish tradition and values.

Each of the various practices of the day needs to be measured against these criteria. Therefore, for example, I think that one may schedule a later *davening* on New Year's Day, as is done on Sundays, even if that "celebrates" the day in some way. The later *davening* time can be explained as simply reflecting the fact that most people do not work on January 1 or on any Sunday in America (even though Sunday was selected because it is the day of Christian rest). Waking up a little later than usual when

---

[8] The source for these four basic principles is found in Rema *YD* 178:1, and the commentaries there.

not having to go to work is a rational activity when not working and is thus permitted. Additionally, the idea of making New Year's resolutions, and taking stock of one's accomplishments and failures, does not seem foreign to Jewish tradition, and we can easily support such practices.

On a related note, I think that an employer who owns a business is much better off *halachically*, by giving "New Year's bonuses" to workers, rather than giving "Christmas bonuses." So too, I think that one may go to a New Year's Eve office party when one feels that such conduct is appropriate and is an expected part of the office culture in which one works, and that nothing improper occurs. This is especially true if participating will better safeguard one's economic security or a potential promotion. It goes without saying, however, that all other aspects of *halacha* must be maintained when participating in such events.[9]

[9] Could, under similar circumstances, an office Christmas party also be attended? A few people have suggested to me that even Christmas parties fit into this category of no longer religious, particularly in America, due to their more generic and secular themes, compared to in Europe where Christmas is still far stronger of a theme. This is even more so true for a generic "holiday party." However, this view requires much analysis due to the highly variable sociological factors which often determine the party's religious character. Even if the party were of a more religious character, there would perhaps still be room for leniency in attending, particularly to protect one's job and prevent *eiva* (arousing hatred towards the Jewish people). For more on these leniencies in attending such parties, see *Igrot Moshe YD* 2:117. Of course, the necessity of such attendance should be carefully weighed, with proper *halachic* conduct always enforced. My own intuition is that Christmas parties are still too religious to attend by routine at least in America, other than under dire situations, or where *eiva* is generated. To Americans, a secular celebration of Christmas is counter-intuitive, but this is clearly what has happened, for example in Japan. See "Christmas in Japan" at https://www.whychristmas.com/cultures/japan which notes:

> "Christmas has only been widely celebrated in Japan for the last few decades. It's still not seen as a religious holiday or celebration as there aren't many Christians in Japan. Now several customs that came to Japan from the USA such as sending and receiving Christmas Cards and Presents are popular. In Japan, Christmas in known

Nevertheless, although it is ultimately permitted to participate in such events, I think that Rabbi Feinstein's assertion, that avoiding such things is "the conduct of the pious", should be preferred.

as more of a time to spread happiness rather than a religious celebration."

Addendum to Appendices I-III

Halacha provides a clear framework for assessing whether American secular holidays should be categorized as "religious," such as Christmas, and thus prohibited for celebration, or as "secular," like July 4th or Thanksgiving, and thus permitted. As we have seen, there is also a "middle category" of holidays: those with religious or Christian origins that are now celebrated in a fully secular manner. In such cases, halacha examines whether the celebration has a rational basis or whether its religious origins have been effectively forgotten. If either of these conditions is met, it may be permissible to celebrate such holidays or participate in their observance to some extent. It is important to note that there is an element of cultural subjectivity in determining whether a holiday's religious origins have entirely disappeared. These matters are often undocumented or difficult to verify precisely. In cases involving holidays with religious roots, it seems reasonable to place the burden of proof on those who assert that the holiday's religious associations have been erased in the culture we currently inhabit.

Finally, although not previously stated in this section, it goes without saying that fully secular holidays—such as Independence Day, Labor Day, and Memorial Day—would be permissible under the approach that allows for the observance of New Year's Day. Whether various federal holidays are philosophically (or hashkafically) worthy of celebration is beyond the scope of this book, though it is evident that many federal holidays emphasize values and ideals that are not only consistent with but also supported by Jewish tradition.

Appendix IV:

Is Turkey a Kosher Bird?

Throughout this book, it has been assumed that eating turkey as a kosher bird is permissible year-round. Indeed, the current practice among nearly all Jews is to treat turkey as kosher, and no kosher certifying organization refrains from certifying turkey as a kosher bird. However, a closer examination of the *halachic* literature reveals that classifying turkey as kosher is not straightforward, with a few earlier authorities even arguing against its kosher status. Clearly, if one were to conclude that turkey is not kosher, it would significantly impact the ability to include it in a Thanksgiving meal.

To assess the kosher status of turkey, we must first clarify what determines a bird's kosher status.[1] Unlike land animals, for which the Torah provides signs to identify kosher species, the Torah does not specify signs for kosher birds. Instead, it lists 24 bird species that are non-kosher.[2] Notably, this list does not represent an exhaustive catalog but rather 24 broad categories of forbidden birds.[3] Thus, any bird not fitting into these categories is considered kosher by default. However, a challenge arises in classifying birds into these categories, as many biblical names remain ambiguous. While some identifications are relatively secure—for instance, the *atalef* is generally understood to be a bat—most are far less certain, raising a key question: how can we reliably determine which birds are permissible?

---

[1] *Leviticus* 11 begins this list for land animals.

[2] *Leviticus* 11:13-19; *Deuteronomy* 14:11-18 cites a slightly smaller list. For a reconciliation of the two lists see *Chullin* 63a.

[3] *Chullin* 63b contains a discussion on this topic, with one view stating there are one hundred birds contained within the single biblical category of *ayya*.

This issue was already pertinent in antiquity, prompting the Sages to discuss additional criteria for identifying kosher birds.

> "The Mishnah in *Chullin* (59a) states: 'The signs of domestic and wild animals were stated in the Torah, but the signs for birds were not. However, the Sages stated: Any bird of prey is non-kosher, and any bird that has an extra toe, a crop, and a peelable gizzard is kosher.'"

The *Rishonim* are divided on how to use these new signs in determining a bird's *kosher* status. While several interpretations exist, the most relevant is from Rav Moshe bar Yosef who understands that if a bird has all three positive signs it is also automatically non-clawing (non-predatory) and thus *kosher*.[4] Many other *Rishonim* concur, including Ramban, Ran, and Razah.[5] While this implies that one need only find all three listed signs in a bird to label it as *kosher*, there is an additional stringency presented by Rashi which Rema takes into consideration.[6] The Talmud cites an example of a predatory, *non-kosher* bird that was mistaken as non-predatory and *kosher* due to possessing other signs of being a *kosher* bird; Rashi uses this to argue that it is best to simply rely on *mesorah* and not use physical signs at all when one is uncertain of a bird's predatory status.[7] This view was then adopted by Rema.[8] Hence, even with methodological ways of determining a bird's *kosher* status, the

---

[4] *Beit Yosef* YD 82:3, *Shulchan Aruch* YD 82:2-3 and *Aruch HaShulchan* YD 82:11-12.

[5] *Beit Yosef* YD 82:3, *Aruch HaShulchan* YD 82:11-12, and Rabbi Avi Zivotofsky, "Is Turkey Kosher?" at https://www.kashrut.com/articles/turk_part2/ footnote 18.

[6] For more on why this minority stringency was adopted see: "Why do we need a *Mesorah* for Birds?" – by Rabbi Natan Slifkin https://www.rationalistjudaism.com/p/why-do-we-need-a-mesorah-for-birds

[7] Rashi on *Chullin* 62b s.v. *chazyuah dedarsah ve'achlah*.

[8] YD 82:3.

codified *halacha* in the time of Rema was for Ashkenazim[9] to only rely on *mesorah* in determining a bird's *kosher* status. This presents a problem of how the turkey could ever have become *kosher* since it was brought from the New World and thus lacked any prior *mesorah*.

Turkeys were likely first brought back from the New World by Spanish Conquistadors around 1519, and by 1524 they had reached other European countries such as England. Ironically, the Thanksgiving Pilgrims who went to the Americas in 1620 brought their turkeys with them from Europe.[10] One major issue that arose with the turkey's arrival in Europe was the various misnomers it was labeled as. In England, the name "turkey" was assigned due to the Turkish merchants who originally sold it. Most other countries, meanwhile, labeled it based on the misidentification of the Americas as India. Hence, even today the turkey is called *tarnagol hodu* in Hebrew,[11] with many later *poskim* labeling it as such and using this as a post-facto justification for its *kosher* status by arguing that Indian Jews must have had the *mesorah*.[12] During this time, many Jewish communities began consuming it and it was only several centuries later that many *poskim* began to more carefully examine the

[9] See *Yalkut Yosef* (*Maachalot Asurot*) YD 82 which argues that the majority view for Sephardim is to not follow Rema on this requirement of a *mesorah*. However, Rabbi Dr. Ari Zivotofsky based on a reading of *Shulchan Aruch* YD 82:2-3 proposed that even Rabbi Karo would agree that a *mesorah* is required albeit with slightly different requirements; for his argument see Is Turkey Kosher? https://www.kashrut.com/articles/turk_part3/ and footnote 23 of this appendix. The problem with Zivotofsky's view, however, is that Rabbi Karo also cites an additional sign of *kosher* status from Razah, known as "the goose exception," in YD 82:3 which weakens the argument that Rabbi Karo always requires a *mesorah*.

[10] "Is Turkey Kosher?" https://www.kashrut.com/articles/turk_part5/

[11] *Hodu* being the Hebrew word for the country/region of India. The Yiddish word *hendika hen* also means Indian chicken.

[12] *Shut Mei Be'er Siman* 19, *Kaf HaChaim* YD 82:21. See also *Yalkut Yosef* cited above. Of course, this view is very difficult to justify as turkey is an American bird and there could be no old *mesorah*.

turkey's true country of origin and began asking how it could ever have entered the Jewish *halachic* diet.[13] After all, while the turkey does have all three *kosher* signs, Rema's insistence on *mesorah* had also been in force; how could this bird have somehow circumvented that issue?

Indeed, Rabbi Shlomo Kluger ruled that no New World birds could be eaten since they cannot possess a *mesorah*.[14] In contrast, the *Arugot HaBosem* argues that both Rema and Rashi's insistence on *mesorah* only applies when the bird's predatory status is uncertain, however, if the bird has been observed regularly and does not exhibit predatory behavior, this concern is nullified.[15] Therefore, since turkeys had already been raised for several centuries without such behavior, it merely required the other signs of being a *kosher* bird, which it did possess.[16] A broader reason for permitting turkey is given by Netziv, who argues that since turkey is now so widespread in its consumption, there should not be any objections leveled at it unless there is strong, explicit evidence that it is *non-kosher*.[17] This is in line with the principle that God would not allow the Jewish people to all sin at once[18] in combination with the idea that an accepted practice should not be so easily reversed.[19]

However, both of these latter answers only worked because by then turkey had been consumed for centuries prior; how then could it have initially *halachically* circumvented Rema's requirement? One theory

---

[13] "Turkey, the Traditionless *Kosher* Bird" - by Natan Slifkin https://www.rationalistjudaism.com/p/turkey-traditionless-kosher-bird

[14] *Ha'Elef Lecha Shlomo* 1:YD:112.

[15] This argument seems especially convincing since Rashi's primary reason for the reliance on a *mesorah* seems to be the uncertainty of identifying a predatory bird. See Rashi *Chullin* 62b s.v. *chazyuah dedarsah ve'achlah*.

[16] Rabbi Aryeh Lebush Bolchiver, *Shem Aryeh, Kuntras Ha-Teshuvot Siman* 16.

[17] *Meshiv Davar*, YD 22.

[18] *Halachot Ketanot* 1:9 quoted by *Tzitz Eliezer* 11:36.

[19] *Shut mi-Ktav Sofer* YD 3-4.

is that the original carriers of Turkey to Europe were Spanish and Turkish, hence Sephardic Jews were the first to encounter the turkey. They perhaps relied on the majority of *Rishonim* who only required the presence of *kosher* signs and ignored the lack of a *mesorah*,[20] and by the time it entered other Ashkenazic European environments, those Jews were aware of prior communities who ate it.[21] Regardless of how the turkey first became consumed by Jews, and regardless of how later *poskim* began to justify its *kosher* status, a simple fact remains: the turkey is evidence of a bird whose *mesorah* was generated only several centuries ago yet still became accepted.

Today, the near universal normative practice in America, Israel and Europe, adhered to by all the major *kosher* certification organizations and the overwhelming majority of observant Jews, is to view turkey as a *kosher* bird fit for consumption throughout the year according to *halacha*. It is not necessarily true that if turkey were to have only been discovered today it would be deemed *kosher* by the Ashkenazic world,[22] rather it was the unique combination of historical circumstances and *halachic* flexibility that produced the *kosher* status of a bird now widely enjoyed.

---

[20] *Otzar Yisrael* as cited by R. Liebes.

[21] See also Shach YD 82:9 for how a reliable *mesorah* can override other concerns.

[22] Rema's insistence on a *mesorah* would likely have been far more binding alongside Rabbi Kluger's concerns for New World birds lacking precedent. However, perhaps Ashkenazim could have still permitted the turkey today; as this is hinted at by Rabbi Ovadia Yosef cited above. Since Sephardim will consider a bird kosher based on signs without a tradition, it might very well be that Ashkenazim can develop a tradition based on Sephardim eating turkey, who are doing so based on the presence of *simanim*. However, there is some 'bootstrapping' in that model.

Appendix V

Teshuva Of Rabbi Ephraim Greenblatt[1]

Rabbi Ephraim Greenblatt
5556 Barfield Road
Memphis, Tennessee 38120
Telephone (901) 682-3291
Fax (901) 685-0258

Michael J. Broyde

Thursday, Week of *Parasha Devarim* 5755,
To the honorable Matityahu Broyde *shlit"a*:
I received your letter today and I was happy to hear from you.

I asked the question to my teacher and master, Rabbi Moshe Feinstein z"l regarding eating turkey on Thanksgiving, and his answer once [was that he] permitted it. I **also asked Rabbi Menashe Klein** *shlit"a*.[2] I will only ask other authorities, when I record my own opinion in my upcoming printing of *Shu"t Rivevot Ephraim* on *Yoreh Deah*[3] that it is permitted to eat it because it is merely a day of giving thanks and not, God forbid, a day of idol worship. That is how I always answer [to those who ask me]. There is a rabbi who disagrees with me but many permit it. I will search [to see] if [perhaps] I have written and received a response from other authorities, in which case I will send it you *bli neder*.

When I purchased the book *Nefesh HaRav*, I saw that the Rabbi from Boston [Rabbi J. B. Soloveitchik] z"l permits it, and I was happy [to see] that I thought like him. If you quote me, note that I permitted this almost thirty years ago.

I then spoke to a close friend of Rabbi Eliezer Silver z"l and he also said that it was permitted.

I received the article on the discussion of the laws of separating *terumot* and *ma'asrot*, and *bli neder* it will take me some time to examine it, but I will write back if I have what to add.[4] Please send me a fax to let me know that this letter was received. Otherwise, I will have to send the letter via post.

Do you have my books, *Shu"t Rivevot Ephraim*? If you do not and are interested, I can send you volume six, of which there are a few

---

2   Rabbi Greenblatt did not write here what Rabbi Klein's response was, however, it was later published in *Mishneh Halachot* 10:116, also found in Appendix X.

3   Which was never published.

4   This is a reference to an article I published that I sent him a draft of. See Michael J. Broyde, "Tithing Fruit Exported from Israel," *Ohr Hamizrach* 43:1–2 (*Tishrei–Tevet* 5755 [Fall 1994]), 21–35 (Hebrew).

remaining, and volume one, of the second edition, which I recently reprinted in Jerusalem.

My apologies for the brevity. I will wait for your response regarding this letter and then will write more, *bli neder*. I will also write on other topics that require clarification.

>Best Regards,
>With Torah Blessings,
>Waiting for your response,
>
>Efraim Greenblatt

יום ה' פ' דברים תשנ"ד

כבוד מתתיהו ברויד שליט"א, אחדשה"ט,

היום קבלתי מכתבו, ושמחתי לשמוע מכת"ה,

אני הוא השואל למו"ה הרה"ג ר"מ פיינשטיין זצ"ל בעניין התרנגול הודו בטענקגיוויננג ותשובתו בעם התורה

וכן אני הוא השואל להגאון ר' מושה קליין שליט"א,

לא שאלתי לגדולים אחרים אלא כשאני לעצמו לכשאדפיס שו"ת רבבות אפרים על יורה דעה כתבתי שדעתי הוא שמותר לאכול את זה כי זה רק אם הודאה ולא ח"ו ע"ז, וכך אני עונה תמיד, חוץ מרב אחד שיצא לחלוק עלי אבל רבו המתירים, אבל אחפש אם כתבתי וקבלתי תשובה מעוד פוסקים אז אשלח לך בל"נ. וכעת כשקניתי ספר נפש הרב ראיתי שהרב מבוסטון זצ"ל מתיר. ושמחתי שכיונתי לדבריו, ואם יכתוב מזה, יכתוב דעתי שהתרתי זה כמעט מלפני ל' שנה עד היום, ואז דברתי עם ידידי הרה"ג ר' אליעזר סילבר זצ"ל וג"כ אמר שמותר. קבלתי המאמר בדין הפרשת תרומות ומעשרות וכו' ובל"נ יקח לי זמן ואעיין שם ואכתוב אם יהי' מה להעיר.

בבקשה שלח לי פעקס שמכתב זה נתקבל אחרת אצטרך לשלוח המכתב בדאר.

האם יש לך הספרים שלי שו"ת רבבות אפרים אם אין לו ומעוניין אז אוכל לשלוח לו ח"ו שנשאר מעט וח"א שהדפסתה כעת בירושלים במהדורה שניה,

סליחה על הקיצור, ואחכה לתשובה על מכתב זה ואז בל"נ אכתוב עוד ויוכל לכתוב בעניינים אחרים הטעונים לו ביאור.

הדו"ש הטוב

בברכת התורה,

המחכה לתשובתו,

אפרים גרינבלאט

Appendix VI

Letter From Rabbi Yitzchak Hutner[1]

Pachad Yitzchak Letters and Correspondences 109:

My dear friend, peace and blessing,

Your letter arrived today, and I have hastened to reply because I am concerned that in this judgement you have a trace of "a time-bound positive *mitzvah*" [to give my answer immediately for your benefit].

About your question [regarding celebrating Thanksgiving], if this is a biblical or rabbinic [violation], behold this entire investigation would not have been [important] if it was judged [to be] in the category of a one-time festival. But since we have here before us a fixed festival that returns every year, via the calendar, thus you have in this the topic of an appointed festival time. And celebrating this day is [now] automatically [considered to be] joining in an appointed celebratory time. And creating an appointed celebratory time whose source is not from the *Torah* – this is the severest [prohibition]. And all of this is correct even if this celebratory time was fixed according to our [Jewish] calendar: this would also [constitute] the severest [prohibition], (and see above). But since it was established according to the customary [Christian calendar] date, from then on [the widespread use of the Christian calendar] it was always our custom to add [the Jewish numerical dates] in the times of

---

[1] Rabbi Yitzchak Hutner (1906-1980) was the famed *rosh yeshiva* of Yeshiva Chaim Berlin in Brooklyn from 1940 until his passing. His writings are collected in numerous volumes of *Pachad Yitzchak*. The intellectual history of this letter is somewhat unknown and even the direct connection to Thanksgiving might be in dispute. Some editions entitle this letter as being about Thanksgiving and others do not. Notice, perhaps, by implication, that Rabbi David Cohen is less certain if Rabbi Hutner really opposed Thanksgiving celebrations in his letter to me found in Appendix IX.

the official use of the [Christian] dates. Is the essence of the fixed [solar calendar] not to serve the foundation of [worshipping Christianity!?][2] It is giving honor [to] idolatry, behold this is a simple matter [to understand] for all intelligent people. Thus, an appointed festival which is established by a fixed [Gentile calendar] date carries [the prohibition of being] ancillary [to idolatry].

In all of this, the publication of these simple matters [this severe prohibition] (see above), [we are] forced to [consider] the knowledge of the majority [of secular society], [like what] we find with the Sages who were concerned [that pronouncing severe prohibitions on Gentile festivals] would cause great *eiva* (hatred towards Jews). This was a great [factor] in the [Sages'] practices, and they reasoned that a great *eiva* from the nations of the world to the Jewish people would be included in the presumption of *pikuach nefesh*[3] [that to save lives and prevent this hatred, such prohibitions should not be pronounced].[4] So of course, I didn't hide

---

[2] Indeed, Rabbi Hutner correctly identified that the current Gregorian calendar has its roots in Christian belief. The original motivation for this calendar was an effort to make sure that the timing of Easter would remain accurate every year. Furthermore, both before and within this calendar, the continued usages of B.C. (Before Christ) and A.D. (The Year of our Lord) to designate the years is quite Christian. Today, however, and dating back even to the 17th century with Johannes Kepler, the terms B.C.E. (Before the Common Era) and C.E. (Common Era) are used in an effort to universalize the calendar for other faiths as well. This, in combination with the almost universal acceptance of the Gregorian Calendar for civil affairs despite many users not being Christian, serves to rebut Rabbi Hutner's claim that today the calendar is still expressly Christian. For more on this see: https://www.worldhistory.org/article/1041/the-origin--history-of-the-bcece-dating-system/

[3] The principle that saving a life negates even biblical prohibitions.

[4] There is a dispute, of weighty importance, whether concerns of "hatred" only allow rabbinic violations or even biblical ones. See Tosfot, *Avodah Zarah* 26a s.v. *savar rav yosef* where it is written that *eiva* only allows one to violate a rabbinic prohibition and not a biblical one. For more on this, see *Encyclopedia Talmudit, Eiva*, 1: at page 493.

from you the obvious truth [that a prohibition exists], but you from your [perspective] in your position, [should] know and be wise [enough] to weigh the [ramifications of the] publication of these things, with [wise] council and knowledge.

2. About your second question [about Thanksgiving practices], I am not an expert in these customs and laws of their ceremonies. But, I do know one [practice], and this is a solid principle which nothing departs from: all the customs and all the new [holidays], [no matter how seemingly secular], all] come from these [idolatrous] sources that you recognize in your letter; [they] sprout from similar [idolatrous] forms to the nations of the world, and automatically all who separate from them are like ones who are joined to life. And the opposite [is also true], all who join to them it is as if they separate from life. The reality of the matter is, it is necessary to distance yourself from these [idolatrous] customs, and [customs that resemble them], and [even from customs that resemble those resemblances]. But I need to repeat the words I said earlier that all these matters are difficult [to share publicly]. [However], the truth [of the prohibition] is [nevertheless] simple and obvious. But according to the conditions and to the times you need [a great] practical ability in how to apply these [rulings].

I am quickly sending this letter, I am sealing it with blessing and love, And peace to you and all which is yours,

Yitzchak Hutner

Michael J. Broyde

פחד יצחק אגרות וכתבים אגרת קט

יחס ליום חגיגה נכרים (טהנקסגיווינג) לגר בין נכרים

יקירי חביבי, שלום וברכה!

מכתבך הגיעני היום, והנני ממהר להשיב מפני החשש כי הנידון יש בו שמץ של "הזמן גרמא".

על אודות שאלתך אם זה דאורייתא או דרבנן, הנה כל החקירה הזאת לא תתכן אלא אם היה הנידון ענין של חגיגה חד - פעמית. אבל מכיון שיש כאן לפנינו קביעות של חגיגה החוזרת מדי שנה בשנה, ונכללת ע"י כך במחזור השנה, הרי יש בזה ענין של מועד. והחוגג את היום הזה בעל כרחו שהוא משתתף במועד. וחידוש מועד שלא ממקורותיה של תורה - הוא מן החמורי חמורות. וכל זה היה נכון אפילו אם קביעות זו היתה לפי הלוח שלנו, גם אז היה העניו מחמורי חמורות, כנ"ל. אבל מכיון שקביעות זו היא לפי התאריך הנהוג, אשר מאז ומעולם היה המנהג אצלנו להוסיף את התיבה "למספרם" בשעת השימוש הרשמי בתאריך הנ"ל, והלא עצם קביעות התאריך לעובדא היסודית של... הוא מתן כבוד עצום לעבודה זרה, הרי מילתא דפשיטא היא לכל בן דעת, כי חגיגת מועד הקבוע לפי תאריך זה יש בו משום אביזרייהו...

בכל זאת, פרסומם של הדברים הפשוטים הנ"ל זקוקה היא לשיקול דעת מרובה, כי כן מצינו בחז"ל שהחשש של איבה היה גורם גדול בהנהגתם. והיינו שסברו כי הגדלת האיבה של אוה"ע לישראל יש בה גררא חזקה של פקוח נפש. ועל כן כמובן שלא העלמתי ממך את האמת הברורה כמו שהיא, אבל אתה מצדך במקומך תדע ותשכיל לשקול את פרסום הדברים במועצות ודעת.

ב) על אודות שאלתך השניה אינני בקי בטיב המנהגים ובהליכות הטכס שלהם. אבל אחת אני יודע, וזה הוא בכלל מוצק מבלי יוצא מן הכלל, כי כל הנהגה וכל חידוש היוצא ממקורות הללו שאתה מזכיר במכתבך צומחים הם מתאות הדימוי לאוה"ע. וממילא כל הפורש מהם כמחובר אל החיים. ולהיפך, כל המתחבר להם כאלו פורש מן החיים. ולאמיתו של דבר, צריך להתרחק מן המנהגים הללו ר"ל, ומן הדומה ומן הדומה לדומה. אבל שוב עלי לחזור על הדברים הנ"ל כי כל זה היא לקושטא דמילתא. האמת הפשוטה והברורה. אבל לפי התנאים ולפי הזמן צריך הרבה פקחות מעשית כיצד להשתמש בהם.

ממהר אני בשלוח המכתב כנ"ל,

הנני חותם בברכה ובאהבה, ואתה שלום וכל אשר לך שלום, יצחק הוטנר.

Appendix VII

Teshuva of Rabbi Feivel Cohen[1]

[Blessings of] life and peace to the honorable Rabbi Matityhu Broyde *shlit"a*,

Attached is a photocopy of a letter that my master and teacher OB"M (Rabbi Yitzchak Hutner) wrote regarding celebrating Thanksgiving Day.[2]

I wish to add an additional point. It appears, in my humble opinion, from the words of Maimonides (*Laws of Kings* 10:9), that [even] a Gentile who celebrates [Thanksgiving] Day has the *halachic* status of a Gentile

---

[1] Rabbi Feivel Cohen (1925-2022) was the author of the acclaimed series *Badai HaShulchan* on *Yoreh Deah* and was a prominent authority of Jewish law in Brooklyn.

[2] Rabbi Yitzchak Hutner, *Pachad Yitzchak: Igrot uMichtavim Shel HaRav Hutner* (5751), 109, found above in Appendix VI. Rabbi Hutner discusses the prohibition of a Jew celebrating any Gentile holiday that was established on a fixed calendrical day, which he sees as being ancillary to idolatry and the editor of the volume in some editions connected this to Thanksgiving.

who [halachically observes Shabbat] who is liable for the death penalty.³ This [is implied] from that which [Maimonides] wrote there that [how much more so should this penalty apply] if [a Gentile] establishes a holiday for himself. This is directly relevant to the aforementioned discussion [with Rabbi Hutner, that even a secular, fixed Gentile holiday is forbidden] as [such celebration] is also included in that which is written, "Day and night they shall not [rest]" (*Genesis* 8:22).⁴ [This phrase means that for the Gentiles,] no distinction may be made between different days to prefer one over the other in establishing a holiday and festival. Therefore, in addition to [the reasons for the prohibition to celebrate Thanksgiving] written in the aforementioned letter [by Rabbi Hutner], certainly one has to [also] refrain from participating in [a celebration] regarding which the founders are in violation of a capital sin.⁵

With blessings,

Shraga Feivel Cohen

---

3   It is worth noting that Maimonides then states that this death penalty as well as the following ones are to be told to the violating Gentile but that they should not actually be executed over these actions.

4   This verse is used by Reish Lakish to derive the above prohibition of a Gentile fully observing *Shabbat*. See *Sanhedrin* 58b.

5   In my opinion, the argument that Thanksgiving celebrations are prohibited to Gentiles according to Maimonides is not completely persuasive. Even if Thanksgiving is a holiday in the American legal sense, it is not at all clear that the manner it is celebrated fits into the *halachic* category of festival (*mo'ed*) or of resting (*shabbat*). It is more of a commemoration than a festival. Indeed, the prohibition for a Gentile to observe *Shabbat*, or any day of rest on any day of the week for that matter, is immediately dismissed when the Gentile deviates in any way from the normative Jewish manner of observing *Shabbat*. As such, as soon as the Gentile turns on a light or drives a car he is not considered to be "resting" any longer. For more on this, see Rabbi J. David Bleich "Observance of *Shabbat* by Prospective Proselytes" *Tradition* 25(3) 46-62 (1991). One could easily claim that the same is true for a Gentile observing Thanksgiving which bears no resemblance to the traditional *Shabbat* and holiday observances.

החיים והשלום למעלת כבוד הרב מתתיהו ברויד שליט״א

רצוף בזה צילום של אגרת שכתב מו״ר זצ״ל (הרב יצחק הוטנר) בעניין חגיגת יום טענקסגיווינג.

ורצוני להוסיף בזה עוד נקודה דנלע״ד מדברי הרמב״ם בהל׳ מלכים פרק י׳ ה״ט שהנכרי החוגג את היום הנה הוא בדין עכו״ם ששבת חייב מיתה והוא מדכתב שם שאם עשה מועד לעצמו חייב מיתה והוא ממש נידון הנ״ל שגם זה נכלל במש״כ יום ולילה לא ישבותו שאין לחלק בין הימים ולהעדיף האחד על חבירו בעשות מועד וחג, ולכן נוסף על מש״כ באגרת הנ״ל בודאי שיש למנוע מלהשתתף במה שאצל המחדשים של החג ההוא הוא עון מיתה.

בברכה

שרגא פייוול כהן

Appendix VIII

Teshuva of Rabbi Yehuda Henkin[1]
Published in *Shu"t Bnei Banim* 3:37 with only small changes

---

[1] Rabbi Yehuda Herzl Henkin (1945-2020) was the leading student of his grandfather, Rabbi Yosef Eliyahu Henkin; he grew up in New York, attended Columbia for College and moved to Israel. He is the author of the widely acclaimed series of responsa entitled *Bnei Banim* and a leading authority in the Religious Zionist community in Israel.

[Holding a Meal on Thanksgiving Day][2]
Blessed be God, 23 *Tevet*, 5755
To my friend Rabbi Matityahu Broyde *shlit"a*,[3]
Atlanta, USA
After inquiring about his [honor's] welfare and well-being,

I only lately had the time to respond to your letter, my apologies. In my humble opinion, it is not prohibited to set later prayer times in the synagogue on the morning of Thanksgiving Day in the United States since everyone knows that the reason [for doing so] is that the day is a vacation day from work and not [in honor] of the cause of the vacation [the events which Thanksgiving Day commemorates]. Therefore, even on Christmas Day, which is a religious holiday, it is not prohibited [to set later prayer times]. But, nonetheless, it is appropriate not to delay the [set] prayer time on that day at all to demonstrate that we do not participate in their holiday at all. On both days [Thanksgiving and Christmas], one should not set the prayer time to its Shabbat designated time. It is also permitted to schedule weddings for Thanksgiving Day.

Regarding [celebrating] Thanksgiving Day itself and consuming turkey in a [festive] meal – in accordance with the custom of the majority of the Jewish people today to view it as a *kosher* bird even though there is no continuous inter-generational tradition about it – [they are] not prohibited because of [the prohibition of] not following Gentile customs even according the view of the Gra[4] since the concept of thanksgiving is a concept written in the *Torah* and consumption of turkey is a mere remembrance for the [reason] of [this] thanksgiving. This [reason] is relevant to the general populace and not only to Christians. Therefore,

---

[2] This title only appears in the published version in *Bnei Banim* 3:37.

[3] As was Rabbi Henkin's style, in the published version, the name of the questioner was left out. The Hebrew text of the teshuva in taken from the Bar-Ilan Responsa project, version 31.

[4] Who insists on a Gentile practice appearing in the Torah with respect to Jews in order to allow it to be followed, see Gra *YD* 178:7.

the reasons I wrote in [my responsa] *Bnei Banim* (2:30) are relevant here too.

In the responsa *Igrot Moshe* (*E.H.* 2:13), [the author – Rabbi Moshe Feinstein] did not [discuss] scheduling a [festive] meal in honor of Thanksgiving Day, [he] only [discussed] scheduling a [Jewish] *mitzvah*-related [festive] meal on that day [such as a wedding]. He wrote that [it is permissible] since [Thanksgiving Day] is not considered a religious holiday. [This responsum] is referenced in the responsa *Mishneh Halachot* (10:116) in which [the author – Rabbi Menashe Klein] quotes [the *Shulchan Aruch*] Y.D. (148:7): "[Concerning] a Gentile who makes a holiday for himself and thanks [his] deities and praises them, such as [on] his birthday or the day he shaves his beard and the locks of his hair or the day he was safely returned from a sea voyage It is only prohibited [to do business with him] on that day and with that person alone…" Meaning, this is considered his [personal] religious holiday. Based on this, [Rabbi Klein] was concerned that Thanksgiving Day is [considered] a religious day since the Gentiles thank their deity and violate [the prohibition concerning] worshiping a non-monotheistic conception of God. Therefore, a Jew should not participate in [such festivity], (see [*Mishneh Halachot* 10:116 for more]). However, he withdrew his opinion in deference to [the aforementioned] view of Rabbi Moshe Feinstein that Thanksgiving Day is not considered a religious holiday.[5] In truth, I do not understand the original view of [Rabbi Klein] since Thanksgiving Day is not comparable to the day that [an individual Gentile] was born or the day that he shaves his beard, etc. since all of those events are festive occasions for the Gentile alone and they have no relevance to Jews. It would have been more relevant to challenge [celebrating Thanksgiving] from Paragraph 6 (*Shulchan Aruch* ibid.) [where it states:] "the day on

---

5   While Rabbi Henkin believes that Rabbi Klein's original view was withdrawn in deference to Rabbi Feinstein, Rabbi Klein's statement of deference could also be construed as simply a colloquialism of humility in the face of a *Torah* giant. See *Mishneh Halachot* 10:116, found in Appendix X, for Rabbi Klein's full letter on this topic.

which the Gentiles gather to appoint an official and they offer sacrifices and praise their deity has the status of a religious holiday" [on which it is prohibited to do business with Gentiles who celebrate it]. [The phrase] "an official" is [a general term] [since] the same would apply to a king, and that [word, "king",] is what appears in Tractate *Avodah Zarah* 10a and in Maimonides and in [the] *Levush*. Perhaps it was changed to "official" because of censorship. Certainly, the day they appoint a king is a day of festivity for all the citizens of that kingdom including the Jews residing there. The same would be relevant for the king's birthday. And even though [it has relevance to Jews], [they] are considered religious holidays [and thus prohibited]. Therefore, the same should apply to Thanksgiving. [even though it has relevance to Jews, its celebration should be prohibited.] However, this is difficult since we have [no source] to prohibit rejoicing on the king's birthday and [during] similar events. The practices of the Jewish people throughout the generations proves [there is no such prohibition]. Rather, [we must conclude that] there are two separate laws. On a [Gentile] religious holiday, it is prohibited to purchase from and sell to Gentiles since they offer sacrifices to idolatrous deities [on that day]. [Regarding] this, it is of no relevance to us what the reason [behind the establishment] of the holiday is. Even the [coronation] day of the king and his birthday are prohibited [if celebrated religiously]. By contrast, regarding [Jews] rejoicing and [practicing] festivity alone there is a distinction. [Regarding] a day on which a primary religious holiday was established based on [worship of] their deity consistent with the formulation of *Tur*, a [contemporary] example being Christmas Day, it is prohibited to participate at all [in any celebration]. But regarding that which was established based on other considerations, and the holiday is primarily of a civil nature, it is permitted to celebrate on it, examples being the [coronation] day of the king, or the Fourth of July in the United States and Thanksgiving. Regarding this [latter category of secular celebrations], it is of no relevance to us that [some] Gentiles worship their deity specifically on those days as well.

In the article in the *Am HaTorah* periodical which his honor sent, Rabbi Moshe Feinstein OB"M permitted scheduling a [festive] meal on Thanksgiving Day as a non-obligatory meal. He wrote that if one does not establish [such a meal] as an obligation and *mitzvah*, one can [schedule it] for a subsequent year as well. Afterward, he wrote that it is prohibited to establish a fixed day in the year to celebrate. He mentioned [that this violates the prohibition of] adding to the *Torah*. The implication [of his words] is that it depends on the intent [of the celebrant] and that there is no objection to celebrating it every year as optional, just that [the celebrant] should not view it as an obligation. And [based] on this perspective of permitting [a celebration], in my humble opinion, you have to skip the meal one out of every few years in order to demonstrate that [this celebration] is not obligatory on him, and [by doing] this, [he] would satisfy any concern.

Concerning the view of *Bach* ([Y.D.]178), see there [where he writes]: "[Concerning] the practices explicitly mentioned by our Sages OB"M in [the fifth chapter] and the *Tosefta* of [Tractate] *Shabbat* and in other places, even though the Gentiles no longer practice them nowadays anywhere, it is prohibited for Jews to practice them, since they originally were established based on their [Gentile] religion, it appears as if [the Jew] is consenting to them and to their religion if he follows those [Gentile] customs which were established in an earlier era." This [ruling] is not relevant here [to the celebration of Thanksgiving]. In the final analysis, that which most Gentiles practice for idolatry one must prohibit even if it was originally permitted such as a [single–stoned] altar mentioned in the Torah. But that which the majority [of Gentiles] do for their enjoyment and it was not idolatrous originally and [the practice] has a [logical] reason, it is of no concern to us if a minority of devout Christians practice it for their religion. This is the case concerning Thanksgiving Day.

With respect,

Yehuda Herzl Henkin

Michael J. Broyde

שו"ת בני בנים חלק ג סימן לז

עריכת סעודה ביום הודיה לאומית

ב"ה, כ"ג טבת תשנ"ה

לרב אחד

התפניתי באיחור למכתבו ואתו הסליחה. לע"ד אינו אסור לאחר את זמני התפילה בבית הכנסת בבוקר של 'חג ההודיה' בארה"ב, כי הכל יודעים שהסיבה היא החופשה מעבודה שבאותו יום ולא מה שגורם לחופשה. ולכן אפילו ב'חג המולד' שהוא יום אידם אינו אסור, אבל מכל מקום ראוי שלא לאחר התפילה ב'חג המולד' כדי להראות שאין לנו חלק ונחלה ביום אידם, ובזה ובזה אין ראוי להשוות זמני התפילה לזמנה בשבת. וכן מותר לקבוע חו"ק ביום ההודיה

. לעצם 'חג ההודיה' ואכילת תרנגול הודו, וכפי מנהג רוב ישראל היום להחזיקו כעוף כשר אף על פי שלא בא במסורת מדור דור, אינו אסור משום בחוקותיהם אפילו לדעת הגר"א, כיוון שרעיון ההודיה הוא עניין הכתוב בתורה, ואכילת תרנגול הודו הוא זכר בעלמא לסיבת ההודיה, והסיבה שייכת לכלל האזרחים ולא רק לנוצרים, ולכן הטעמים שכתבתי בבני בנים חלק ב' סימן ל' שייכים גם כאן.

ובשו"ת אגרות משה חלק אבן העזר חלק שני סימן י"ג לא התיחס לע- שיית סעודת 'חג ההודיה' רק לקביעת סעודת מצווה שלנו באותו יום וכתב שאינו בגדר יום אידם, ומשם לשו"ת משנה הלכות חלק י' סימן קט"ז שה- ביא מיורה דעה סימן קמ"ח סעיף ז': "עובד כוכבים שעושה הוא חג לעצמו ומודה לאלילים ומקלסה ביום שנולד בו, ויום תגלחת זקנו ובלוריתו, ויום שעלה בו מן הים וכו' אינו אסור אלא אותו יום ואותו האיש בלבד" עב"ל, כלומר דהוי יום אידו, ומזה חשש שיום ההודיה הוא יום אידם כיוון שה- נכרים מודים בו לאמונתם ועוברים על שיתוף ולכן אין לישראל לקחת חלק בו עיין שם, אמנם ביטל דעתו בפני מה שיורה הגרמ"פ ז"ל והגרמ"פ הלא כתב שאינו יום אידם. ובאמת לא הבנתי דברי שו"ת משנה הלכות כי יום ההודיה אינו דומה ליום שנולד בו ויום תגלחת זקנו וכו' שכל אותם המאורעות הם שמחת הגוי בלבד ואין לישראל חלק בשמחה זו, ויותר היה לו להקשות מסעיף ו' שם: "יום שמתכנסים בו העובדי כוכבים לה- עמיד להם שר ומקריבים ומקלסים לאלהיהם יום חגם הוא" עב"ל, ושר לאו דווקא אלא הוא הדין מלך וכן הוא במסכת עבודה זרה דף י' עמוד א' וברמב"ם ובלבוש ואולי נשתנה לשר משום הצנזורה, ובוודאי יום שמ- עמידים בו מלך הוא יום שמחה לכל בני הממלכה גם ליהודים שבתוכה,

Jewish Law and the American Thanksgiving Celebration

וכן יום הולדתו של מלך, ואף על פי כן הוי יום אידם ולכן הוא הדין ליום ההודיה'. ברם הוא תמוה כי היכן שמענו שאסור לשמוח ביום הולדתו של המלך וכיוצא בזה ומעשים בכל הדורות יוכיחו, אלא ישנם שני דינים נפרדים, כי ביום אידם אסור ליקח מהם ולמכור להם כיוון שמקריבים לע"ז ובזה לא איכפת לן מה הוא טעם חגם ואפילו יום העמדת המלך ויום הולדתו אסור, מה שאין כן לעניין שמחה וחגיגה בלבד, יש חילוק כי יום שהוא עיקר האיד שהחזיקו בו ועל שם אלוהיהם כלשון הטור ולדוגמה חג המולד אסור ליטול חלק בו כלל, ואילו שאר איד שהחזיקו בו ועל שם שאר דברים ועיקרו חג אזרחי מותר לשמוח בו, ולדוגמה יום הכתרת המלך או הרביעי ביולי בארה"ב ויום ההודיה, ובזה לא איכפת לן שהנכרים פולחים לאמונתם גם באותם הימים.

ובמאמר בחוברת "עם התורה" ששלח כבודו התיר הגרמ"פ ז"ל לעשות סעודה ב'יום ההודיה' בתור סעודת הרשות וכתב: "שבלי קביעת חובה ומצוה יוכל גם לשנה אחרת", ושוב כתב: "שאסור לעשותה יום קבוע בשנה לחוג זה" והזכיר בל תוסיף, ומשמע שמיירי בכוונת הלב, ושאין מניעה מלעשותה רשות מדי שנה רק שלא יראה אותה כחובה. ועל הצד היותר טוב לע"ד יש להמנע אחת לכל כמה שנים מעשיית הסעודה כדי להראות שאינה חובה עליו ובזה יצא מידי כל חשש.

בדעת הב"ח בסימן קע"ח נא עיין שם, וז"ל: "אותן הדברים המפורשים בדברי חכמים פרק במה אשה ובתוספתא דשבת וביתר מקומות אף על פי שאין העבו"ם נהוג בהם עכשיו במקצת מקומות אסור לישראל לנהוג בהם דכיוון שכבר היה קבוע חוק זה לשם תורה שלהן נראה כמודה להן ולתורתן אם נוהג כאותן מנהגים שהיה חוק מקדם" עכ"ל, ואינו עניין לכאן. סוף דבר מה שרוב גויים עושים אותו לשם ע"ז יש לאסרו גם אם מעיקרו היה מותר וכמו מצבה שבתורה, אבל מה שהרוב עושים להנאתם ואינו ע"ז מעיקרו ויש בו טעם, אזי לא איכפת לנו אם נוצרים אדוקים עושים גם אותו לשם דתם וכזה הוא 'יום ההודיה'!

יהודה הרצל הנקין

Appendix IX

Letter of Rabbi David Cohen[1]

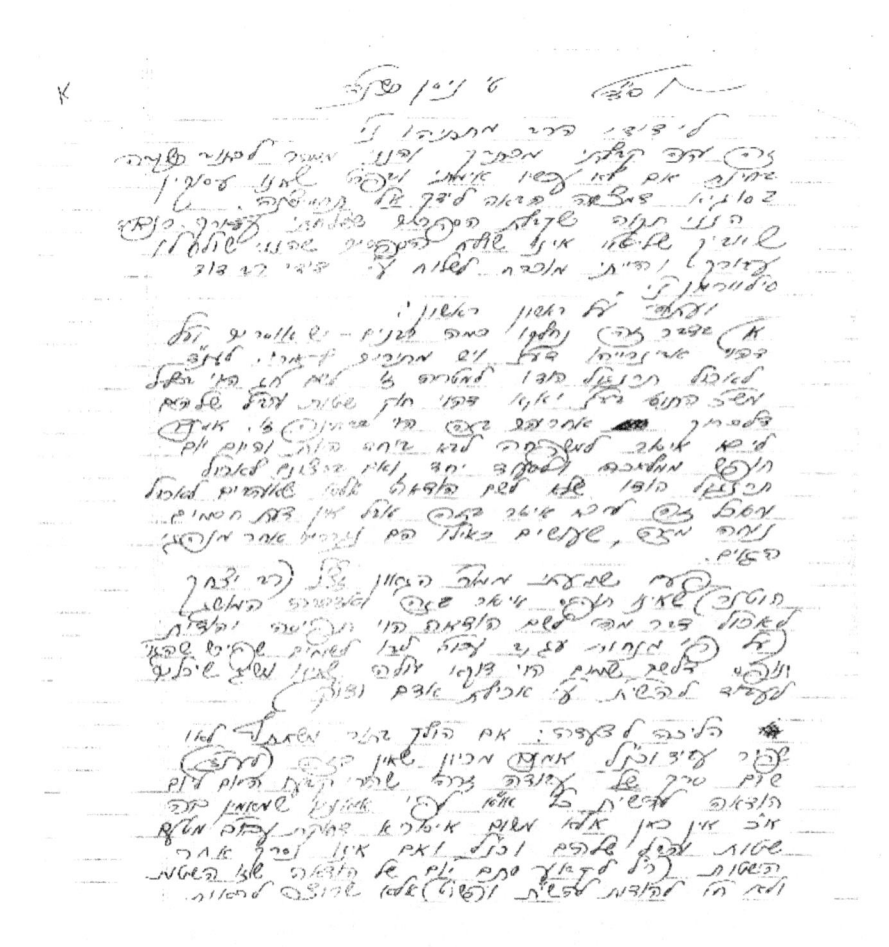

---

[1] Rabbi David Cohen (b. 1932) resides in Brooklyn and is one of the leading authorities on Jewish law in America today. He is the author of many volumes of rabbinics, from commentary to analysis and responsa under the titles *Yavetz* and *Ohel David*.

Jewish Law and the American Thanksgiving Celebration

9th of Nissan, 5755

To my friend Rabbi Matityahu, may he live long,

I have now received your letter and I am quickly penning a reply, [this is a] test [for fulfilling the injunction] "If not now, when," [Pirkei Avot 1:14] [especially since] we are [currently] learning the [halachic] topic of "A commandment that comes your way, do not delay it!"[2]

I hope you have received the books I sent for you. It appears that your father, may he live long, is not sending the books that I send to him for you,[3] and I had to send [them] via my friend Rabbi David Silverman, may he live long.[4]

Now [to answer your questions] in order:

1) Concerning this matter [the celebration of Thanksgiving Day], there is a dispute between several Rabbinic authorities. Some prohibit [it] and maintain that [such celebration] is considered ancillary to idolatry [and therefore is severely prohibited], [while others] permit [it] completely. In my humble opinion, to consume turkey for this purpose, [namely] for the sake of the holiday, is included in [one of the categories of prohibited Gentile customs], which Tosfot ([Tractate] *Avodah Zarah* 11a) mentions, since [Thanksgiving] is a nonsensical, meaningless practice of theirs. Following [the Gentiles] in this matter is included in

---

[2] This letter was sent before *Pesach* in which Jews customarily learn the related laws of the holiday. *The Mechilta* expounds on the verse "And you shall watch over the *matzot*" (Exodus 12:17), reading the word not as *matzot* but as *mitzvot* (the difference of inserting just one extra letter *vav*), to mean that just as you must make sure the *matzah* does not leaven and become ruined, you must also not delay the performance of a *mitzvah* that comes your way.

[3] My father, Rabbi Dr. Barry (Chaim Dov) Broyde ז״ל was a study partner with Rabbi Cohen for many years, starting when my father was a student in Chaim Berlin, Rabbi Hutner's Yeshiva.

[4] Rabbi David Silverman is the Dean of the Atlanta Scholar's Kollel. I was learning in that Kollel during afternoon seder at that time. Rabbi Silverman was going in the summers to Camp Munk, where Rabbi Cohen was in residence, and Rabbi Cohen must have given Rabbi Silverman books to give to me.

this [prohibition]. However, there is no prohibition for the family to get together and dine together, since the day is a day off from work. If they wish to eat turkey not for the sake of Thanksgiving, but because they like [turkey], there is no prohibition. However, the Rabbis would not be pleased with this, since they are acting as if they are following Gentile customs.

Once I heard from my teacher and master, the genius *OB"M* (Rabbi Yitzchak Hutner) that he does not view [eating turkey in honor of Thanksgiving] as prohibited. On the contrary, the concept of eating something for the sake of thanksgiving is [only rooted in] a Jewish perspective. (Based on [Tractate] *Menachot* 73b: "The non-Jew's heart is toward heaven." [Rabbi Hutner] explained [this to mean] that the non-Jew maintains that [acting] "for the sake of heaven" is expressed [exclusively] regarding an *olah*-sacrifice [one fully consumed by the altar]. [The non-Jew] does not comprehend that it is possible to serve God, blessed be He, through human[s] eating [a sacred meal as well] Note this well.)

[Concerning] going to the [Thanksgiving Day] Parade: If one goes as a participant [to the festivity], it is not permissible as mentioned above [since it violates the prohibition of imitating Gentile customs]. However, since (in my humble opinion) this does not entail any concern of idolatry in light of the fact that they established this day as a day of thanksgiving to God, blessed be He, [for] each person according to his [particular] beliefs to which he subscribes, consequently, the only prohibition is one of following Gentile customs which are nonsensical and meaningless, as mentioned above. If [his intent] is not to follow th[is] nonsensical [custom], ([to follow it would] mean establishing a random day of thanksgiving which is nonsensical, and God forbid to not [even do so], to thank Gd, blessed be He; this point is obvious [that it is forbidden]), but rather he wishes to [merely] watch the parade, then, on the contrary, [watching] any parade (except for idolatrous ones) constitutes a fulfillment of the directive of our Sages *OB"M* who permitted a Rabbinic form of defilement[5] as stated in [Tractate] *Berachot* (19b): "We used to leap over coffins of the deceased… to see Gentile kings, etc."[6]

However, I state strongly that all of this, [merely watching the parade], is only relevant to adults, but [regarding] the youth, where [there is a concern] that they will [mistakenly] understand that it is proper to join the other citizens of the country to celebrate this day, it is not at all proper, and this constitutes improper education concerning following nonsensical, Gentile customs.

(As an aside, in my humble opinion, it would appear that the prohibition of following Gentile customs connected to idolatry, and the prohibition of following a nonsensical, meaningless custom are derived from different [Biblical] verses. This is not the place to elaborate [on this point].)[7]

2) It would appear that there is no prohibition to schedule an event such as a wedding or an ordinary meal, such as a friendly get-together, as

---

[5] *Chazal* were especially focused on promoting the laws of ritual purity both on a biblical level and on a rabbinic level. Indeed, much of *The Talmud* is dedicated to long discussions about these topics as well as discussing interactions with Jews who do not scrupulously keep them.

[6] This *Talmudic* statement was said by Rabbi Elazar bar Tzadok, who was a priest, which demonstrates the significance of this principle, as priests specifically are required to not come into any ritual contact with the dead.

[7] Despite not elaborating on this point, it is my view that Rabbi Cohen is attempting to make a connection between Maimonides and Tosfot on Gentile customs. Maimonides cites multiple Biblical verses as the sources for prohibited Gentile customs in his *Laws of Idolatry* Chapter 11:1, yet he does not distinguish between categories of Gentile customs like others such as Tosfot do. The fact that Maimonides stated multiple prooftexts indicates to Rabbi Cohen that Maimonides would agree with Tosfot that there are different categories of prohibited Gentile customs, and that he disagrees with Ran and Maharik who only feel there is a single category of idolatrous customs. Further proof to this interpretation of Maimonides is that within this section of *Mishneh Torah*, he cites both idolatrous and non-idolatrous Gentile customs. For more on these different positions, see section IV in the main book.

long as the participants are not doing so in order to join in the festivity of [Thanksgiving] Day. This only applies if the youth understand that there is no [intent] to join [in the festive celebration of the day], as mentioned above.

3) In my humble opinion, one should be careful not to change the [established] prayer time even on [an ordinary] Sunday. This is what we do in our synagogue [keeping the same time everyday]. (Perhaps one can permit an additional [service] at a later time so that late-comers can pray with a quorum, but to change the established prayer time because of the [Gentile] holiday is not proper.) However, I cannot state that there is a formal prohibition in doing this since it is difficult to identify a specific prohibition. But it is clear that the Rabbis would not be pleased with this [behavior].

4) I do not think there is any difference [to my rulings] if there are Gentiles present too. I also do not think there is any difference [to my rulings] if there are religions who celebrate [Thanksgiving] Day as part of their religion since the [original] "holiday" was established in a manner that all could celebrate and that each religion individually would celebrate that day as a day of thanksgiving, as mentioned above.

A Happy and *Kosher* [*Pesach*],

David [Cohen]

בס"ד

ט' ניסן תשנ"ה

לידידי הרב מתתיהו נ"י

זה עתה קבלתי מכתבך והנני ממהר לכתוב תשובה בחינת אם לא עכשיו אימתי ובפרט שאנו עסוקין בסוגיא דמצוה הבאה לידך אל תחמיצנה.

הנני תקוה שקבלת הספרים ששלחתי עבורך. כנראה שאביך שליט"א אינו שולח הספרים שהנני שולח לו עבורך והייתי מוכרח לשלוח ע"י ידידי רב דוד סילווורמן נ"י.

ועתה על ראשון ראשון:

א) בדבר זה נחלקו כמה רבנים – יש אוסרים וס"ל דהוי אביזרייהו דע"ז ויש מתירים לגמרי. לענ"ד לאכול תרנגול הודו למטרה זו לשם חג הוי בכלל מש"כ התוס' בע"ז י"א,א דהוי חוק שטות והבל שלהם דלברוך אחריהם בזה הוי בחינה זו. אמנם ליכא איסור למשפחה לבא ביחד היות והיום יום חופש ממלאכה ולסעוד יחד, ואם ברצונם לאכול תרנגול הודו שלא לשם הודאה אלא שאוהבים לאכול מאכל זה ליכא איסור בזה אבל אין דעת חכמים נוחה מזה, שעושים כאילו הם נגררים אחר מנהגי הגוים.

פעם שמעתי ממו"ר הגאון זצ"ל (רב יצחק הוטנר) שאינו תפוס איסור בזה ואדרבה המושג לאכול דבר מה לשם הודאה הוי תפיסה יהודית (על פי מנחות ע"ג,ב עכו"ם לבו לשמים שפירש שהגוי תופס דלשם שמים הוי דוקא עולה שאינו משיג שיכלים לעבוד להשי"ת ע"י אכילת אדם ודו"ק).

הליכה לצעדה: אם הולך בתור משתתף לאו שפיר עביד וכנ"ל אמנם מכיון שאין בזה (לענ"ד) שום סרך של עבודה זרה שהרי קבעו היום ליום הודאה להשי"ת כל או"א לפי אמונתו שמאמין בה א"כ אין כאן ולא אלא משום איסורא דחוקת עכו"ם מטעם שטות והבל שלהם וכנ"ל ואם אינו נסרך אחר השטות (ר"ל לקבוע סתם יום של הודאה שזו השטות ולא ח"ו להודות להשי"ת ופשוט) אלא שרוצה לראות בצעדה אז אדרבה יש בכל צעדה (חוץ משל ע"ז) קיום של מצות חז"ל שהתירו טומאה דרבנן ובהא דברכות י"ט ב מדלגין היינו ע"ג ארונות של מת... לקראת מלכי עכו"ם וכו'.

אמנם הנני אומר בתקיפות שכל זה למבוגרים אבל להמשיך צעירים שיתכן שהם יתפסו להתתתף עם שאר בני המדינה לחוג יום זה אז אי"ז נכון כלל יש בזה משום חינוך שלא לנהוג כמנהג שטות של גוים.

(ואגב לענ"ד נראה שהאיסור של הליכה בתר חוקות גוים שיש בזה משום עבודה זרה להליכה בתר חוק שטות והבל שלהם למדים מפסוקים שונים

111

ואכמ"ל.)

ב) נראה דליכא איסור לעשות שמחה כמו חופה וגם לעשות סעודת רשות כמו סעודת מריעים כל זמן שאין המשתתפים עושים כן מטעם הצטרפות לחגיגת היום. ובמה דברים אמורים שהצעירים יבינו שאין בזה השתתפות וכנ"ל.

ג) לענ"ד יש להקפיד שלא לשנות זמן תפילה גם ביום ראשון וכן נוהגים אצלנו בבית מדרשינו. (אולי יש להתיר מנין נוסף בזמן אחר כדי שהמאחרים יוכלו להתפלל במנין – אבל לשנות זמן המנין קבוע מפני יום אידם אינו נכון.) אמנם איני יכל לומר שיש איסור בזה שקשה לבאר שם האיסור אבל ברור שאין רוח חכמים נוחה מזה.

ד) איני רואה שום נפ"מ בזה אם ישנם גם נכרים. גם איני רואה שום נפ"מ אם ישנן דתות שחוגגים היום בדתם כיון שנקבע ה"מועד" באופן שהכל יחוגו וכל דעת כשלעצמה תחוג היום כיום הודאה וכנ"ל.

חג כשר ושמח

דוד

Appendix X

Teshuva of Rabbi Menashe Klein[1]

Published in Mishneh Halachot 10:116

Is there a Prohibition of Eating Turkey on [Thanksgiving]

5th day of the Torah portion "Abraham fathered Isaac," [*Toldot*] 5741, New York.

To my distinguished and beloved friend, the renowned scholar, the famous veteran and pious crown of *Torah*, our teacher and our master, [Rabbi] Ephraim Greenblatt *shlit"a*, author of the three-volume *Rivevot Ephraim*.

Greetings to you in true friendship.

The beginning of the legal matter of a person who asked about the *halachic* opinion concerning someone who wishes to publicize that eating turkey on the holiday of Thanksgiving constitutes a clear prohibition, [even] being included [in the prohibition of] "you will be killed and will not transgress"[the obligation to forfeit one's life rather than violating prohibitions concerning idolatry]. While [this man] does not wish to permit [celebrating Thanksgiving at all], nevertheless [he is concerned] that issuing such a [severe] prohibition in [this] free country, [where] this holiday symbolizes liberties which we benefit from [too], could lead to [the Gentiles] resenting us if this prohibition were to be announced. It might be interpreted as showing ingratitude for the freedoms we benefit from, possibly [even violating the prohibition of] "the law of the land."[2]

---

[1] Rabbi Menashe Klein (1924-2011) was the author of an 18-volume series of responsa on Jewish law entitled *Mishneh Halachot*. He was also known as the Ungvar Rav after the Brooklyn Chasidic community he led. The Hebrew text of the teshuva in taken from the Bar-Ilan Responsa project, version 31.

[2] A *halachic* principle that in matters of the local government's civil law, within certain parameters, Jews are required to obey them.

Michael J. Broyde

You concluded your letter [by mentioning] that last week you spoke to the [master], the great Rabbi Moshe Feinstein *shlit"a* (may God grant him a full recovery) about this.

First, my dear friend, I am sorry that you did not include Rabbi Feinstein's opinion [in your letter]. Regardless, what did the [great] master say, so "how can straw be compared to grain" [*Jeremiah* 23:28]?![3] If [the master] has already provided a ruling or opinion, it should be heeded.[4] Perhaps you meant to follow the principle explained in the *Nimmukei Yosef* (*Sanhedrin* 36), [which was] brought by Rema (*Y.D.* 242), which states that one should not mention the greater scholar's opinion first so that the lesser scholar is not reluctant to offer his view in the presence of the greater scholar. Therefore, [you wisely] did not tell me what the master said so that I would be able to write to [you] what is on my mind [my view of this matter].

Regarding [your concerns of violating] "the law of the land" or [causing] "resentment" [by announcing a severe prohibition of Thanksgiving], I do not know [if this is enough] to prevent us from issuing [such a] Torah opinion: if there was indeed a prohibition [in the celebration of Thanksgiving] [as severe as] "you will be killed and will not transgress," we would not worry at all about it being their holiday [and possibly causing resentment by rejecting it]. They have many [other] holidays, and God forbid we should celebrate them [to avoid such concerns]. Also, in matters involving [a violation of] our holy Torah, we are not concerned with violating "the law of the land." (see *Shach* on *C.M.*

---

[3] A humble colloquialism: how can Rabbi Klein give his opinion in the face of a *Torah* giant such as Rabbi Feinstein?

[4] As noted in Appendix VIII, Rabbi Henkin indeed felt that Rabbi Klein did retract his view in deference to Rabbi Feinstein. However, based on the continuation of this letter, this phrase could also be taken as a colloquialism of humility in the face of a *Torah* giant.

356:10[5], where he questions Rema['s opinion] that "the law of the land" does not apply if it contradicts the Torah.)[6] (Also see in my own work *Mishneh Halachot* 7:84, on the topic of observing [Gentile] holidays, that this is a complete prohibition. [Furthermore], the celebrations that they make for themselves, are included [in the prohibition of Gentiles observing their own fixed holidays]. See Maimonides Chapter 10 from *The Laws of Kings*, Halacha 9, "a Gentile who studies the *Torah* is liable for the death penalty,[7] and so a Gentile who observes *Shabbat*, even on a weekday, if he made [a *shabbat*] for himself [observing all the laws of *shabbat*] he is liable for the death penalty, and [how much more so should this penalty apply] if he makes a religious festival for himself.

---

5 Shach in CM 356:10 refers to his objection to Rema found at CM 73:39, where Shach objects to Rema's deference to a civil court concerning selling property, due to the applications of "the law of the land," leading to his lengthy discussion of when that law applies. See also Rema's formulation of these limitations in CM 369:11. It is important to note that both Rema and Shach agree that if "the law of the land" contradicts the *Torah* it does not apply; their argument is merely on the application of that principle.

6 Rabbi Klein's point here is that if the act of celebrating Thanksgiving would truly violate the prohibition of "you will be killed and not transgress," then it is incumbent on the community to publicize this; the concern for causing Jewish hatred or violating the government's laws do not take priority in such a situation. Thus, the man's concerns in publishing his prohibitive view about Thanksgiving are not a problem. See Appendix VI where Rabbi Hutner seems to think publicizing such a view does require more consideration. Nevertheless, as Rabbi Klein will go on to say in the next paragraph, he does not believe such a severe prohibition is included in Thanksgiving celebrations.

7 It is worth noting that Maimonides then states that this death penalty as well as the following ones are to be told to the violating Gentile but that they should not actually be executed over these actions.

The general principle of these laws is they cannot make a new religion or make religious commandments for themselves from their own views..."[8]

Nevertheless, regarding their Thanksgiving holiday, according to my humble opinion, this does not fall under "you will be killed and will not transgress," [but rather only the prohibition stated by *Shulchan Aruch*] Y.D. 178[:1] that one should not follow the customs of Gentiles. Tosfot on *Avodah Zarah* 11a states that there are two types of [prohibited] Gentile customs:

1. Those that are performed for nonsensical or superstitious purposes, which the *Torah* [does not write that we should do], [lest] we learn from [the *Torah* that it is actually permitted].

2. Those that are performed for idol worship which we find [written] in the *Torah* to not do these practices. For example, in [Tosafot] Sanhedrin 52b [sv *ela*], that pagan priests would shave their beards, and thus the Torah prohibited such. See also Rambam in Chapter 12 of the Laws of Idolatry and the comments of MaHarsha [on YD 178:1].

Rema [however], explains [Y.D. 178:1] that "Gentile practices are only forbidden if they are for the purpose of immorality, such as wearing scarlet clothing [which] signifies nobility and similarly immodest clothing, or if there is no reason behind the practice, [which leads] to [the] concern that it carries the prohibition of "the ways of the *Emorites*"

---

[8] In my opinion, the argument that Thanksgiving celebrations are prohibited to Gentiles according to Maimonides is not completely persuasive. Even if Thanksgiving is a holiday in the American legal sense, it is not at all clear that the manner it is celebrated fits into the *halachic* category of festival (*mo'ed*) or of resting (*shabbat*). It is more of a commemoration than a festival. Indeed, the prohibition for a Gentile to observe *Shabbat*, or any day of rest on any day of the week for that matter, is immediately dismissed when the Gentile deviates in any way from the normative Jewish manner of observing *Shabbat*. As such, as soon as the Gentile turns on a light or drives a car he is not considered to be "resting" any longer. For more on this, see Rabbi J. David Bleich "Observance of *Shabbat* by Prospective Proselytes" *Tradition* 25(3) 46-62 (1991). One could easily claim that the same is true for a Gentile observing Thanksgiving which bears no resemblance to the traditional *Shabbat* and holiday observances.

[performing superstitious practices which have] a trace of idolatry from their ancestors" (see Gra's lengthy explanation on this [topic], [Y.D. 178:]7) . However, [Rema] writes that only in a [non-promiscuous] practice or statute that lacks any reason [at all], there is a concern for "the ways of the *Emorites*", but in a [non-promiscuous] practice which has [any] reason [this is grounds to permit it]. If [this is true], then [regarding] those who eat Turkey [on Thanksgiving], I heard that this is because [for the historical Pilgrims] there was nothing for them to eat, and they found this bird and rejoiced and gave thanks on [its discovery].[9] Therefore, [since there is a reason for eating Turkey on Thanksgiving] it would not be included in the prohibition of "the ways of the *Emorites*" . However, this practice needs further investigation, as it is [still] connected to their [Gentile] holiday. See [*Shulchan Aruch*] Y.D. 148:7 which states that "if a Gentile makes a personal festival, [which will include] praising their deities, [such as] on their birthday or on the day that they shave their beard, and so forth" [it is prohibited to do business with them that day]; this prohibition could perhaps apply to [Thanksgiving where] Gentiles praise [their deity] [for] the discovery of this bird. They claim to thank God, blessed be He, rather than idols for finding this bird, but in [in their concept of monotheism] there is [the trinitarian concept of God][10] God

[9] Rabbi Klein interprets Rema's opening clause (*YD* 178:1) as the normative *halacha*: that only immoral and baseless acts are included in this prohibition. However, Rabbi Feinstein inferred from Rema's concluding clause, which permits a practice containing a reasonable basis, that any foolish or insignificant basis for a practice is also prohibited. Thus, it seems that Rabbi Klein disagrees with Rabbi Feinstein's interpretation of Rema, preferring to interpret Rema as permitting any modest practice that has an explanation. See Appendix XI for Rabbi Feinstein's full interpretation of Rema.

[10] In response to this type of observation Rabbi J. David. Bleich noted to me that "Thanksgiving was a *seudat hodaah* instituted by Puritans who were absolute monotheists and came to America because they were persecuted for being anti *avodah zarah*. What's the problem?" This is a very important comment. (It is worth noting that the Thanksgiving Pilgrims were not Puritans: Puritans wished

forbid that I know [of such concepts]. If [they are praising a trinitarian God], then it would be included in [the prohibited category] of Gentile holidays [because] they [praise a non-monotheistic God] in the ways of their ancestors. [Given these concerns], certainly this holiday is not appropriate for Jews to join [festively] with the Gentiles, God forbid, and the Rabbis would not approve [of one who does so]. Perhaps there is [even this] biblical prohibition [of celebrating Gentile holidays; but to say that this [holiday] is included in the [severest] prohibition of "you will be killed and not transgress" is not [established]. Note this [last point] well.[11]

Sincerely,

Menashe *HaKatan* [Klein]

to reform the Church of England from within the system while the Pilgrims were "Separatists" who fled England to avoid persecution for leaving the Church. Nevertheless, Puritans and Pilgrims shared the same monotheistic theology, their differences were merely political.) The Pilgrims were not idol worshipers at all, believing in a unitarian concept of God, and were in America to avoid persecution. The theme of Thanksgiving as a holiday of religious freedom has certainly been diminished with the passage of time. It is worth noting that in Rabbi Bleich's view, even if one came to a society where many celebrated Thanksgiving in a pagan way, its origins are not pagan and monotheists can celebrate it properly, no different than if a pagan faith began to celebrate Shavuot, that would not prohibit our celebration.

[11] Rabbi Klein concludes by arguing that while the practice of eating a Thanksgiving turkey meal does have a valid reason, which negates the prohibition of imitating Gentile customs, there is still perhaps a separate prohibition of celebrating Gentile holidays, particularly due to the problematic trinitarian concept of God. Thus, he advises against such practices especially in light of a possible biblical violation.

שו"ת משנה הלכות חלק י סימן קטז

אי יש לאסור אבילת תרנגול הודו (טורקי) ביום חג

ה' לסדר אברהם הוליד את יצחק התשמ"א בנ"י.

מע"כ ידידי ורב חביבי הרב הגאון המפורסם וו"ח כש"ת מוה"ר אפרים גרינבלאט שליט"א בעל מחבר ספר רבבות אפרים ג"ח.

אחדשכ"ת בידידות נאמנה.

תחילת דינו של אדם על ד"ת אשר בקש לדעת חוו"ד העני' באחד שרוצה לפרסם שהאוכל תרנגול הודו (טויקי בלע"ז) ביום חג טענקסגיווינג בלע"ז הוי איסור גמור ובכלל יהרג ואל יעבור ומעכ"ת הגם שאינו רוצה להתיר מ"מ לפרסם דבר כזה במדינה חפשית וחג זה להם סמל לחירות ואנחנו נהנים מהם ואם יצא באיסור כזה יש בזה משום איבה ומראים שאין מכירין טובה עבור החפשיות והו"ל כעין דינא דמלכותא. ובסוף המכתב סיים שבשבוע שעברה הי' אצל הגאון הגדול רבי משה פיינשטיין שליט"א (השית"ש ישלח לו רפואה שלמה מן השמים) ושוחח עמו עבור זה עכ"ל.

וראשונה ידידי מאד אני מצטער שלא כתב לי חוו"ד הגרמ"פ שליט"א ועכ"פ מה שאמר בזה מרן הגאון שליט"א כי מה לתבן את הבר אם הוא אמר לו איזה פסק או חוו"ד אליו תשמעון ואולי כוונתו לפ"מ דמבואר בנמק"י סנהדרין ל"ו והובא ברמ"א יו"ד סי' רמ"ב וכן פסקו האחרונים דאין לומר דעת הגדול קודם שמא הקטן לא ירצה עוד לומר דעתו נגד הגדול ולכן שכל את ידיו ולא הגיד כלל מה שאמר הגאון שליט"א כדי שאוכל לכתוב לו מה שעל לבי.

והנה מטעם דינא דמלכותא או מטעם איבה לא ידעתי אי משום זה יש לנו למנוע מלכתוב דעת תורה ואם באמת היה בזה איסור עד כדי יהרג ואל יעבור לא היינו חוששים כלל שלהם הוא חג, והרבה חגאות יש להם וח"ו לנו לחוג בחגאות שלהם וגם מה שנוגע לתורתינו הקדושה לא חוששין לדין של דינא דמלכותא עיין ש"ך ח"מ סי' שנ"ו סק"י מה שתמה על הרמ"א שם דלא אמרינן דד"מ דינא מה שהוא נגד התורה ועיין בספרינו משנה הלכות ח"ז סי' ע"ד ובפרט לענין לשמור חג שלהם שהוא איסור גמור ובפרט בחגאות שעושים לעצמן שהוא בכלל עובדי דת לעצמו עיין רמב"ם פ"י מהל' מלכים ה"ט עכו"ם שעסק בתורה חייב מיתה וכן עכו"ם ששבת אפילו ביום מימות החול אם עשאוהו לעצמו כמו שבת חייב מיתה ואין צריך לומר אם עשה מועד לעצמו כללו של דבר אין מניחין אותו לחדש דת ולעשות מצות לעצמן מדעתן וכו' ע"ש.

ומיהו לעצם הענין לפענ"ד ליכא בזה דין דיהרג ואל יעבור והנה ביו"ד סי' קע"ח אין הולכין בחוקת עובדי כוכבים ולא מדמין להם וכתבו התוס' ע"ז י"א א' דתרי חוקי עו"כ יש א. שעושים להבל ולשטות וכזה אין כתוב באורייתא עושים דלאו מינייהו גמרינן, ב. שעושין לעו"כ וכזה שמצינו בתורה אין עושין כמנהגם וכ"כ בסנהדרין נ"ב ב' דרך כהני עו"כ הי' להשחית זקנו לפיכך אסרה התורה להשחית זקן עיין רמב"ם פי"ב מה' עו"ז והביאו בגליון מהרש"א, וכתב הרמ"א ז"ל דלא אסור אלא בדבר שנהגו בו עו"כ לשם פריצות כגון שנהגו ללבוש מלבושים אדומים והוא מלבוש שרים וכדומה לזה ממלבושי הפריצות או בדבר שנהגו למנהג וחוק ואין טעם בדבר דאיכא למיחש ביה משום דרכי האמורי ושיש בו שמץ עו"כ מאבותיהם ועיין ביאור הגר"א אות ז' שם מה שהאריך הרבה.

הנה כתבו דדוקא דבר שנהגו למנהג וחוק ואין טעם בדבר איכא למיחש משום דרכי האמורי אבל בדבר שנתנו טעם לדבר הרי טעמו בצדו א"כ בהני שאוכלין תרנגול כפי ששמעתי הוא משום שלא הי' להם לאכול ומצאו אותו העוף ושמחים ונותנים שבח על שמצאו העוף לכאורה אין זה בכלל חוק משום דרכי האמורי אלא דמ"מ יש לעיין בזה מטעם חג ועיין יו"ד סי' קמ"ח ס"ז עו"כ שעושה הוא חג לעצמו ומודה לאלילים ומקלסה ביום שנולד בו ויום תגלחת זקנו וכו' וכיוצא באלו וא"כ אפשר דהאי נמי בגדר זה של עו"כ שמקלסין על שהמציא להם עוף זה אלא שלפי שאומרים הם מודים להשי"ת על זה ולא לעו"כ אלא שגם בזה הרי הם משתתפים ח"ו כידוע וא"כ אפשר דהוא בכלל חגם ומנהג אבותיהם בידיהם ולכן ודאי אין לבנ"י להשתתף עם עכו"ם ביום חגם זה ח"ו ואין רוח חכמים נוחה הימנו ואולי גם אסור מדאורייתא ג"כ אבל לומר דהוה בכלל איסור יהרג ואל יעבור אין לך ודו"ק.

ידי"נ דושכ"ת בלב ונפש. מנשה הקטן

Appendix XI

The Complex and (Perhaps) Contradictory Approach or Approaches of Rabbi Moshe Feinstein[1] Regarding Thanksgiving

Rabbi Moshe Feinstein has four published *teshuvot* (responsa) on the issues related to celebrating Thanksgiving, all of which conclude that Thanksgiving is not a religious holiday, but a secular one. The purpose of this appendix is to translated all of the material found in Rabbi Feinstein's teshuvot and provide some annotation to help the reader understand them.

The first *teshuva*, written in 1953/5723, discusses the deliberate scheduling of weddings and the like on religious holidays of other faiths. Rabbi Feinstein states:

שו"ת אגרות משה אבן העזר חלק ב סימן יג

ובדבר לעשות איזה שמחה בימי איד של הנכרים אם הוא מצד אמונתם, אם בכוונה מחמת שהוא יום איד אסור מדינא ואם בלא כוונה יש לאסור מצד מראית העין, וסעודת מצוה כמילה ופדה"ב יש לעשות אפילו בימי איד שלהן, דאין לאסור בשביל מראית עין סעודה המחוייבת, אבל סעודת בר מצוה טוב לדחות על יום אחר, ואף נישואין יש לקבוע לכתחלה על יום אחר. ויום ראשון משנה שלהם וכן טענקס גיווינג אין לאסור מדינא אבל בעלי נפש יש להם להחמיר.

---

[1] Rabbi Moshe Feinstein (1895-1986) was arguably the foremost Orthodox Jewish legal authority of the twentieth century. Renowned for his profound scholarship and practical wisdom, he resided in New York City from 1937 until his passing, where he addressed complex halachic questions from around the world. His extensive responsa, published in nine volumes under the title Igrot Moshe, cover a vast array of topics and continue to serve as foundational texts in modern halachic discourse.

Michael J. Broyde

Igrot Moshe Even HaEzer 2:13

On the question of celebrating any event on a holiday of Gentiles, if the holiday is based on religious beliefs [by the Gentiles], such celebrations are prohibited according to [Jewish] law if deliberately scheduled on that day; even without intent, it is prohibited because of *marit ayin*[2] . However, a celebration which is a religious commandment such as a *Brit* or *Pidyon HaBen* [ritual redemption of a Jewish son] you have to [celebrate] even on their holidays because there is no reason to prohibit an obligatory celebration due to *marit ayin*; However, [regarding] a *Bar Mitzvah* it is best to delay it to another day and even [for] a wedding you have to set it from the outset on another day. The first day of their year [January 1][3], and Thanksgiving are not prohibited according to

[2] *Marit ayin* is a term used to describe acts which might appear to onlookers as a transgression. A famous example *of marit ayin* is eating or drinking *kosher* food in a *non-kosher* restaurant. So too, when non-dairy creamer and "*kosher* cheeseburgers" first appeared there were some serious concerns for *marit ayin*. Nowadays, however, these foods have become mainstream and consuming them no longer arouses any such suspicions. *Marit ayin* issues change and evolve depending on social norms driven by when is something misunderstood as something else.

[3] The status of New Year's Day has changed in the last hundred years. In contemporary America there is little religious content or expression to New Year's Day, and while there might be many problems associated with the way some celebrate it, few would classify it as a religious holiday. However, Terumat HaDeshen 195, writing nearly five hundred years ago, classifies New Year's as a religious holiday and this is quoted by Rema, *YD* 148:12. Terumat HaDeshen discusses whether one may give a New Year's Day gift and refers to January 1st as "the eighth day of Christmas." He clearly understands the holiday as religious in nature and covered by the prohibition of assisting a Gentile in his worship. (The text of the common edition of the *Shulchan Aruch* here has undoubtedly

the law, but pious people [*baalei nefesh*] should be strict [not to do so].

Thus, we see in this first *teshuva* that Rabbi Feinstein does not consider Thanksgiving to be a religious holiday. Rabbi Feinstein reinforces his understanding that Thanksgiving is not a religious holiday in a *teshuva* published in 1980/5741. He states:

שו"ת אגרות משה יורה דעה חלק ד סימן יא

ד. אם אסור מצד בחוקותיהם לא תלכו, להשתתף בסעודת יום ההודייה שעושים בארצות הברית

ובדבר השתתפות במי שמחשיבים יום ההודייה (טיינקסגיוויינג) כעין חג לעשות בו סעודה. הנה לכאורה מכיוון שבספרי דתם לא הוזכר יום זה לחג, וגם לא שיתחייבו בסעודה, וכיוון שהוא יום זכר לאנשי המדינה, שהוא ג"כ שמח במדינה שבא לגור לכאן עתה או מכבר, לא מצינו בזה איסור לאו בעשיית שמחה בסעודה, ולא באכילת תרנגול ההודו (אינדיק). וכדמצינו כה"ג בקידושין דף ס"ו ע"א שינאי המלך עשה שמחה בכבישה דמלחמה בכוחלית שבמדבר ואכלו שם ירקות לזכר. אבל ודאי אסור לקבוע זה לחובה ולמצווה, אלא לשמחת הרשות עתה. ובאופן זה בלא קביעות חובה ומצווה יוכל גם לשנה האחרת ג"כ לשמוח ולעשות בו סעודה (ועי' עוד בזה להלן סימן י"ב).

אבל אני סובר דמ"מ אסור לעשות יום קבוע בשנה לחוג זה, ורק בשנה ההוא שכבש ינאי המלך, בזה עשה השמחה ולא לקביעות, ויש בה גם משום בל תוסיף, עיין מגילה דף ז' ע"א וברמב"ן בפירוש על התורה דברים על פסוק לא תוסיפו (דברים ד' ב'). ואף שיש לדון לעניין הלאו, מ"מ איסור ודאי הוא זה.

---

been subject to considerable censorship. For an accurate rendition of Rema, see Rema's *Darchei Moshe* in the new edition of the *Tur* published by *Machon Yerushalyim*.). This is perhaps why Rabbi Feinstein in the calendar for *Ezrat Torah* does not list New Year's Day since that calendar was made in the 1930's when New Year's Day was more religious while this teshuva from the 1950's already was in a more secular society. For more on this, see Appendix III.

Igrot Moshe Yoreh Deah 4:11:4

If there is a prohibition of imitating Gentile customs in participating in a Thanksgiving Day meal that is made in America.

On the issue of joining with those who think that Thanksgiving is like a holiday to make a meal: since it is clear that according to their religious law books this day is not mentioned as a religious holiday and that one is not obligated in a meal [according to Gentile religious law], and since this is [only] a day of remembrance to citizens of this country, as well as a [day of] happiness in the country [for] when they came to reside here either now or earlier, *halacha* sees no prohibition in celebrating with a meal or with the eating of turkey. One sees similarly in [Tractate] *Kiddushin* 66a, that King Yannai made a celebration after the conquest of *Kochalit* in the desert and they [the Sages] ate vegetables as a remembrance.

Nonetheless, it is prohibited to establish this as an obligation and religious commandment [*mitzvah*], and it [must] remain a voluntary celebration [at this time]; in this manner -- without the establishment of obligation or religious commandment -- one can celebrate the next year too with a meal. (For more on this see also later in [*Shulchan Aruch Y.D.* 4]: Section 12) But, I think nonetheless, it is prohibited to establish a fixed day in the year for the celebration [of Thanksgiving] since it [was] only in the first year of the event, when Yannai conquered [*Kochalit*], that they had a celebration, and [they did] not [do so] permanently [every year]. There is also a [problem] of adding commandments [to those already in the *Torah*] (see [Tractate] *Megillah* 7a and Ramban on *Deuteronomy* 4:2). Even though one can question the source [of adding anything to the Torah], it is still a real prohibition.

Thus, Rabbi Feinstein appears to also rule here that Thanksgiving is not a religious holiday, and there is no prohibition of celebrating "Gentile holidays" while observing it. Nonetheless, he prohibits its ongoing celebration as an obligation on a particular day because he feels that this would be a prohibited addition to the Jewish calendar and would create a problem of adding commandments to the *Torah*. While Rabbi Feinstein's objections to adding observances will be discussed later, it is clear that he sees no problem in Thanksgiving's celebration as a Gentile holiday, and he appears to see no problem with eating a turkey meal on that day as a matter of choice, and not obligation.

As proof to the fact that Rabbi Feinstein rules that eating turkey is permissible[4], he states elsewhere in the same *teshuva*:

שו"ת אגרות משה יורה דעה חלק ד סימן יא

והנה פשוט לע"ד דאף מה שהוא ודאי נחשב חוק העכו"ם, אם הוא דבר שחזינן שעושין כן כולי עלמא דנכרים, גם אלה שלא שייכי כלל לאמונתם ולחוקותיהם, מטעם שכן יותר ניחא לעלמא להנאתם, כבר ליכא על זה איסור דבחוקותיהם לא תלכו. וגם פשוט שאם יעשו עכו"ם חוק לע"ז שלהם לאכול איזה מין מדברים הטובים והראוים לאכילה - שלא יאסר אותו המין לאכילה. וכמו כן כל הנאה שבעולם, לא שייך שתיאסר בשביל שעכו"ם עשו זה לחוק.

Igrot Moshe Yoreh Deah 4:11:4

Thus, it is obvious in my opinion, that even [in a case] where something would certainly be considered a prohibited Gentile custom, if the general populace of Gentiles do it for reasons unrelated to their religion or law, but rather because it is pleasurable to them, then already there is no prohibition of imitating Gentile

---

4   See Appendix IV where this is noted as the common practice.

customs. So too, it is obvious that if Gentiles were to make a religious law to eat a particular item that is good to eat, *halacha* would not prohibit eating that item. So too, any item of pleasure in the world cannot be prohibited merely because Gentiles do so out of religious observance.[5]

This section indicates that the act of eating turkey can never in and of itself be viewed as a prohibition absent an act of prohibited celebration.

However, in another *teshuva* (also written in 1980/5741), Rabbi Feinstein seems to state that in fact there is a prohibition to celebrate Thanksgiving, even though he acknowledges that Thanksgiving has no religious content. In this *teshuva*, he views such celebratory activity on Thanksgiving as irrational, and thus prohibited as a form of imitating secular society.[6]

שו"ת אגרות משה אורח חיים חלק ה סימן כ

ו. אם מותר לעשות סעודה בטענקס - גיווינג, שהוא יום הודייה של הנוכרים באמעריקא

ובדבר טענקס - גיווינג, כבר כתבתי לאחד בתשובה באג"מ ח"ב דאה"ע סימן י"ג, שאין לאסור מדינא לקבוע על יום זה איזה שמחה, כסעודת בר מצוה ונישואין, אלא שבעלי נפש יש להם להחמיר. אבל לעשות שמחה וסעודה לכבוד טענקס - גיווינג, יש וודאי לאסור מדינא. ולא משום שאיכא בזה חשש דמיון לשמוח ביום איד של

---

[5] Rabbi Feinstein then applies this principle to going bare-headed, and rules that even if some Gentiles do so out of religious fervor, since many people do so out of concerns for comfort, this is not considered a religious custom.

[6] However, a close examination of this letter reveals that the only time Rabbi Feinstein would consider such conduct prohibited is if it was done with celebratory rituals associated with celebrating Thanksgiving, perhaps reciting a text or singing a song, and not merely eating a family meal. It is interesting to note that in 2013 *Hallel* (with a blessing!) was recited on Thanksgiving since it coincided with *Chanuka*. This will occur again in 2070.

ע"ז בנוכרים, שהרי אין יום זה איד שבדו הכומרים, אלא מעצמן עשו שמחה ביום זה. ואף שאז אולי היו הנוכרים שעשו זה עובדי ע"ז, ונתנו שם בדבריהם דברי שבח להע"ז, אינו שייך זה לשנים אחרונות, שאחרים התחילו ג"כ לקבוע סעודות ביום זה, שהם לא שייכי לאיזו ע"ז. וכי כל אדם אף של נוכרים עושה דווקא שמחות לע"ז, וגם הרי בזה"ז רוב שמחות וסעודות שלהם אינם לע"ז. וגם דאין מקריבין קרבנות, וליכא שום תקרובת לע"ז, כמפורש בתוס' ריש ע"ז ד"ה אסור, אף בימי האיד שלהם. ואין דברי התיפלה שאומרין בסעודתן, אוסר מלאכול מצד איסור ע"ז, **אף בנוכרים שעושים זה לכבוד אמונתם. אלא שמה שאסור לעשות שמחה לכבוד יום זה הוא מדין ובחוקותיהם לא תלכו, אף שאין זה חוק לע"ז, אלא חוק הבל ושטות בעלמא.** כדאיתא שאיכא איסור כזה בתוס' ע"ז דף י"א ע"א ד"ה ואי, בסופו.

Igrot Moshe Orach Chaim 5:20:6

If it is permissible to make a festive meal on Thanksgiving, a day of non-Jews giving thanks in America.

Concerning Thanksgiving Day, I have already responded to a questioner in *Igrot Moshe* (*E.H.* 2:13), that halachically it is not prohibited to schedule a festive event such as a *Bar Mitzvah* or wedding meal [on that day], but [that] *baalei nefesh* [those following a stricter standard of observance] should be strict [not to do so]. However, to arrange a festivity and a festive meal in honor of Thanksgiving [Day], is certainly prohibited *halachically*. This is not because of a concern of similarity to the celebration of an idolatrous holiday in the manner of the Gentiles, since [Thanksgiving Day] is not a holiday which [Gentile] priests established. Rather, [the lay population] established a holiday that day. Even if it is possible that the ones who established it were idolatrous and would deliver in their [festive] speeches' words praising the idolatrous deity, this is not relevant to more recent years during which others – who are not connected to any particular idolatrous religion – also have begun to establish festive meals on this day. Do all [non-Jewish] people, even [religious] Gentiles, only [establish] festivities for idolatry?! Even nowadays, most of the festivities and festive meals are not [in honor of] idolatry. No sacrifices are offered, and there is no [other] offering for idolatry as explicitly mentioned by Tosfot (beginning of [Tractate] *Avodah Zarah* [2a] s.v. *assur*) even on their [idolatrous] holidays.[7] Words of nonsense [idolatrous content], delivered at the festive meal do not prohibit participation from the perspective of the prohibition against idolatry **even regarding Gentiles who celebrate in honor of their beliefs. Rather, [the reason] it is prohibited to establish festivity on this day is from the prohibition of "and in their statutes you will not walk" [not following Gentile customs] even though it is not a custom [rooted] in idolatry, but rather a mere frivolous, nonsensical custom [since]** Tosfot writes that this is also [included in that] prohibition ([Tractate] *Avodah Zarah* 11a, end of s.v. *v'ee*).

As demonstrated above, Rabbi Feinstein views any celebratory act specifically intended for Thanksgiving as falling under the prohibition against imitating Gentiles, based on Tosafot's extension of this prohibition to include any frivolous practice, even if secular. In the continuation of this teshuva, Rabbi Feinstein further establishes this as the only prohibition involved in making a festive Thanksgiving meal.

---

7   Tosfot there notes that by their time, idolators did not bring any idolatrous offerings outside of monetary pledges, and hence stricter prohibitions of forbidding interactions during Gentile holidays were not practiced by the Jews in that era.

He clarifies that merely eating turkey on that day—without additional celebratory acts—is not prohibited

ואם איכא מנהג לנוכרים לאכול ביום טענקס - גיוויינג בשר תרנגול הודו (אינדיק), אף אלו שאין עושין סעודה ושמחה שייך לאסור להם עצם אכילת בשר הודו ביום ההוא. אבל לא מסתבר שיהיה אצל נוכרים אינשי בעלמא, איזה חיובים מצד מנהגם, בלא הילולא וחינגא בעלמא. שא"כ אין לאסור אכילת בשר תרנגול הודו בעלמא בלא כוונה למנהגם, אלא משום שיש לו תרנגול הודו, דליכא מראית העין, מאחר שהוא בלא הלולא וחינגא. ומספק אין לאסור לסתם אינשי בעלמא לאכול תרנגול הודו, כשאינו עושה הלולא וחינגא. ומי שאמר שהוא איסור ע"ז, ואיכא על אכילת תרנגול הודו ביום האיד דטענקס - גיוויינג חומרא דיהרג ואל יעבור, לא ידע העובדא. ואף אינו יודע דיני דיהרג ואל יעבור, שגם על אכילת תקרובת עכו"ם, ועל שתיית יי"נ ממש - היינו שנתנסך ממש לעכו"ם - משמע שליכא דין דיהרג ואל יעבור. דהא משמע שאינו עובר בזה על איסורי עבודת ע"ז, אלא על לאו דאיסור מאכלות. דהא ילפינן יין שנתנסך לעכו"ם, מאכילת בשר קרבן שהקריבו לעכו"ם. ובשר הזבח לע"ז, ממת, ומת מעגלה ערופה, בע"ז דף כ"ט ע"ב. משמע שאינו אלא בהלכות מאכלות אסורות, שאסורין גם בהנאה, אבל לא מלאווי עבודת ע"ז. וגם הרמב"ם לא נקטינהו בהלכות ע"ז, אלא בהלכות מאכלות אסורות פי"א, משמע שאין דינם בחומרי עבודת ע"ז. ורק שלענייין השיעור כתב שם הרמב"ם בה"ב, שיש להו חומר ע"ז דאף בכל שהו, עיין שם. ואף על עשיית אותו יום ליום משתה ושמחה, אין לאסור מצד איסורי ע"ז, **אלא איסור חוק נכרים בעלמא**, כדלעיל. וגם באיסור זה אינו ברור ויש לעיין עוד. וע"ע להלן סימן י"א אות ד', וסימן י"ב, מה שהסיק בזה.

If there is a Gentile custom to eat turkey on Thanksgiving Day, even for those who are not making a festive meal and [other] festivity, it is plausible to prohibit eating turkey on that day. But it is illogical that ordinary, lay Gentiles would have [established] specific obligations based on their custom without any festivity or dancing.[8] Based on this, the mere consumption of turkey because one has some is not prohibited [unless one is] specifically intending to follow the [Gentile] custom [of celebrating Thanksgiving]. This is [also] not prohibited because of *marit ayin* [the appearance of wrongdoing] since there is no festivity or dancing. One who declared that [eating turkey on Thanksgiving] is prohibited because of idolatry, and [such consumption is included in] the full stringency of "you will be killed and will not transgress" [the obligation to forfeit one's life rather than violating prohibitions concerning idolatry] does not know the facts. He also does not know the laws of "you will be killed and will not transgress", since even [concerning] the consumption of idolatrous offerings and libation wine, actually libated for idolatry, the implication is that the law of forfeiting one's life rather than violating [the prohibition does not apply]. [The proof to the above is as follows.] The implication is that [one who consumes the aforementioned items] does not violate prohibitions related to actual idolatry [which would require sacrificing your life] but rather [only] a prohibition concerning prohibited foodstuffs. [The prohibition against consumption of] wine libated for an idolatrous deity is derived from the [prohibition against] the consumption of the flesh of a sacrifice offered to [idolatry]. [The latter] is derived from [the prohibition of benefit from] a corpse, and [this is derived] from [the prohibition of benefit from] the *egla arufa* [the decapitated calf brought for an unsolved murder] ([Tractate] *Avodah*

---

[8] Meaning they would not have decreed to just eat turkey without any other celebratory act.

Zarah 29b). The implication [of the above] is that the prohibition [against consumption of idolatrous food] is only [connected to] the laws of prohibited foodstuffs from which any [other form of] benefit is prohibited but [that it] is not connected to the prohibitions of idolatry. Maimonides also did not record these prohibitions [of consumption] in [his] *Laws of Idolatry*, but rather in [his] *Laws of Forbidden Foods* (Chapter 11). The implication [of Maimonides' organization], is that [such consumption] does not have the [more] stringent laws of idolatry [which would require sacrificing yourself]. Only concerning the [requisite] amount [of idolatrous wine consumption which would make you liable to receive lashes], does Maimonides write (ibid. Paragraph 2) that [such consumption] has a stringency] of idolatry, [because] even the smallest amount [is prohibited and would obligate you to receive lashes] (see there [ibid. Paragraph 2]). Even the establishment of the Day [of Thanksgiving] as a day of a festive meal and festivity is not prohibited from the perspective of the prohibitions of idolatry, but **rather only [because] of the prohibition of following Gentile customs** as mentioned above. Even this prohibition [of Gentile customs] is not absolutely clear and requires further analysis. [Original Ed. note: See further [*O.C.*] 11:4 and 12 that which Rabbi Feinstein concludes there.]

Rabbi Feinstein, in his fourth *teshuva* on this topic, clarifies the apparent contradiction in his *teshuvot*, by clearly recognizing that prohibiting any festivities is merely a stricture, as it is predicated on the approach that argues that secular rituals without religious origins are prohibited by the prohibition of imitating Gentiles which he states is not the normative *halacha*, but only a stringency. In this *teshuva*, he states that the responsa block quoted above[9] is to be considered the normative one.

שו"ת אגרות משה יורה דעה חלק ד סימן יב

ביאור המסקנה בתשובות בעניין סעודה שעושים ביום ההודייה דארצות הברית

בע"ה א' דר"ח תמוז תשמ"א.

מע"כ נכדי היקר והחביב לי עד למאד הרה"ג מוהר"ר מרדכי טענדלער שליט"א שלום וברכה לעולם.

הנה עניין יום ההודייה דארצות הברית (טענקס - גיווינג), שזה לא כבר בחודש אייר שנה זו כתבתי (לעיל חלק אורח חיים סימן כ' אות ו') שלעשות שמחה וסעודה לכבוד היום דטענקס - גיווינג יש לאסור מדינא, אף שליכא בזה חשש איסור יום אידיהן, דהא אינו מימי אידיהן שבדו הכומרים, אבל איכא בזה האיסור לאו דובחוקותיהם לא תלכו (ויקרא קדושים י"ח י"ג). ובזמן קצר בתשובה אחרת לחכם אחר (לעיל סימן י"א אות ד'), כתבתי שבעצם לא מצינו בזה איסור לאו, לא בעשיית שמחה בסעודה ולא באכילת תרנגול ההודו (אינדיק). אבל ודאי אסור לקבוע זה לחובה ולמצווה, אלא לשמחת הרשות בפעם זה ובאופן ארעי, כזה יוכל גם בשנה האחרת לעשות כן. ואני מסיק דמ"מ אסור לע"ד לעשות יום קבוע בשנה לחוג זה. ואף בהא דינאי המלך שעשה שמחה וסעודה בכיבוש מלחמה בכוחלית שבמדבר בקידושין דף ס"ו ע"א, היה זה רק בשנה ההיא דכיבש ולא בשנים אחרות. וגם כתבתי שיש בזה משום בל תוסיף, לרמב"ן בפירושו עה"ת פ' ואתחנן (ד' ב') על קרא דלא תוסיפו, ולא הזכרתי שבטעענקס - גיווינג איכא איסור דבוחוקותיהם לא תלכו.

---

[9] See second *teshuva* cited in this appendix, YD 4:11:4.

Igrot Moshe Yoreh Deah 4:12

Clarification of the conclusion of the responsa concerning scheduling a festive meal on Thanksgiving Day in the United States

With the help of Gd, 1st day of *Rosh Chodesh Tammuz*, 5741

His honor, my very precious, dear grandson, Rabbi Mordechai Tendler *shlit"a*, [with wishes of] eternal peace and blessing.

Concerning Thanksgiving Day in the United States, [about which] I have already written this year in *Iyar* (earlier O.C. [5]:20:6) that arranging festivity and a festive meal in honor of Thanksgiving Day is prohibited by *halacha*, even though there is no concern of the prohibition of [celebrating] idolatrous holidays since it is not one of the idolatrous holidays invented by the [Christian] religious leaders, but it is [nonetheless] included in the prohibition of "and in their statutes you will not walk" [not following Gentile customs], (*Leviticus* 18:3). [However,] a short time afterward, in a different responsum to another scholar (earlier [Y.D.] [4]:11:4), I wrote that essentially there is no prohibition, neither in arranging festivity through a festive meal nor in eating turkey. However, [I did say that] certainly it is prohibited to establish this [practice] as an obligation and religious commandment; [it is only allowed] as an optional festivity this time and temporarily. Such [a temporary festivity] one may arrange even in another year. I conclude[d] [there] **that it is nonetheless prohibited – in my humble opinion – to establish a set day of celebration [in honor] of this. Even concerning**

> King Yannai, who arranged a festivity and festive meal over the military conquest of *Kochalit* in the desert ([Tractate] *Kiddushin* 66a), that was only in the year of the conquest and not in subsequent years. I also wrote that [such permanent establishment of a holiday] violates *bal tosif* [adding to *Torah* law], according to Ramban (Commentary to *Deuteronomy* 4:2 on the verse "Do not add...."). I did not mention [in that responsum] that [the celebration of] Thanksgiving is included in the prohibition against following Gentile customs.

After Rabbi Feinstein clarifies that the standard *halacha* is to permit such celebrations occasionally as he wrote in his *teshuva*[10], he then explains that his other *teshuva*[11] which prohibits any festivities is a mere stricture. As support for his stricture, Rabbi Feinstein cites Rema[12] in stating that when something is done by Gentiles and there is no reason for it, we are concerned that this would fall under the prohibition of imitating Gentiles and there could be a trace of idol worship in it. Rabbi Feinstein states, that this position of Rema also applies to any situation where the reason for the practice is not a significant one. However, he clarifies that it is not because there is a concern that the insignificant reason is just to mask an idolatrous, secret reason for the practice, which would make it prohibited. Rather, establishing something for any insignificant reason is itself problematic, and falls within the prohibition of imitating Gentiles.

> הנה מה שעומדת על הסתירה לענין הלאו דובחוקותיהם לא תלכו, וגם מה שהקשית דלהרמ"א יו"ד סימן קע"ח סעיף א' ליכא בכעין זה הלאו. וכוונתך בהא שאיכא טעם

[10] See second *teshuva* cited in this appendix, YD 4:11:4.

[11] See third *teshuva* cited in this appendix, OC 5:20:6.

[12] YD 178:1.

בדבר, שהרמ"א כתב שדבר שנהגו לחוק ואין טעם בדבר
איכא למיחש ביה משום דרכי האמורי ושיש בו שמץ ע"ז.
אבל ברור שאין כוונת הרמ"א שאין בו טעם כלל, שודאי
הוא הדין אף אם יש טעם אבל אינו טעם שכדאי לחדש
בשביל זה איזה מעשים לעשות, שא"כ זה שעושים איזה
דבר לקביעות בשביל זה הוא דרכי האמורי. ואין כוונת
הרמ"א דאיכא למיחש ביה שמא אין עושין זה בשביל
הטעם מאחר שאינו חשוב - אלא משום דיש להם טעם
אחר שאינו ידוע לנו שהוא מעניני כשפים שהן דרכי
האמורי, **אלא כוונתו דלקבוע עשיית מעשים בשביל דבר
שאינו חשוב לידע ולזכור זה - הוא עצמו דרכי האמורי.**

Concerning that which you noticed: the [apparent] contradiction concerning the negative commandment of not following Gentile custo ms as well as that which you challenged that according to Rema (Y.D. 178:1) there is no violation of [this] negative commandment concerning [a celebration] such as this [Thanksgiving]. Your intent, [to challenge that Rema would prohibit Thanksgiving], is [because you believe the prohibition is not] regarding something for which there is a[ny] reason, since Rema wrote that [for] a matter which [the Gentiles] practice as a custom without any reason, there is a [halachic] concern of "the ways of the *Emorites*" [the prohibition against following superstitious Gentile practices] and such [activity] has a trace of idolatry. It is clear, that it is not the intention of Rema that [the prohibited Gentile practice] has no reason whatsoever, since certainly the same would apply even if there is an [insignificant] reason [for the practice], but [the prohibition would] not [apply to] one for which it is appropriate to institute certain rituals to perform. Consequently, that [for] which they do institute some set practice because of this [insignificant reason] has a [concern of] "the ways of the *Emorites*." It is [also] not the intention of Rema that there is a concern that perhaps they are not performing this [ritual] because of the [revealed] reason since it is not significant [enough], but rather that they have another unknown [and concealed] reason which relates to witchcraft which is [included] in "the ways of the *Emorites*."[13]]. **Rather, [Rema's] intent is that the establishment of [any] particular act because of an insignificant event [in order for the people] to know and remember [it] is itself [included] in the "ways of the** Emorites."

Rabbi Feinstein takes this interpretation of Rema,[14] that any Gentile practice with an insignificant reason falls under the prohibition of imitating Gentile customs, and applies it to Thanksgiving, which he viewed as a holiday for which no rational purpose existed. He states that commemorating the fact that the Pilgrims survived and ate turkey due to a lack of other provisions is foolish, as their settlement played no important role in determining whether the country of America would exist. Indeed, he states that food was plentiful in America when the Pilgrims arrived, and they simply had the misfortune of being somewhere where it was more difficult for them to acquire any. Additionally, had the colony failed, other settlers would have simply come from Europe with greater provisions. As a result, commemorating the survival of this colony centuries later with thanksgiving, and celebration, and eating turkey would fall under the category of foolishness.

וזה איכא בעשיית יום שמחה למעשה זו - שאכלו אותן האנשים בבואן למדינה זו ואירע שלא היה להם איזה זמן מה לאכול, ואכלו תרנגולי הודו - שלא היה זה עניין גדול

---

[13] This would mean that if we don't suspect that the insignificant reason is concealing a real idolatrous purpose, it too would be permitted.

[14] YD 178:1.

להתיישבות דאמעריקא. שכבר היה גם אז באמעריקא מה לאכול לרוב אלו שבאו אף אז, והיו כמה מיני פירות וגם עופות אחרים וגם בהמות וחיות ודגים בימים ונהרות. אך שמזדמן לאיזה אינשי שהיו באיזה מקום בזמן שלא היו פירות, וגם היה קשה להם להשיג הבהמות והחיות הגדולות, ואכלו תרנגולי הודו. ואף אם אינשי אלו לא היה להם מה לאכול, מאחר שכבר ידעו בעולם מאמעריקא, היו באים אינשי אחריני באיזו ספינות עם מיני אוכלין ומיני זרעונים לזרוע, והיה מדינת אמעריקא לישוב כמו שנעשה גם בלא זה. שנמצא שלעלמא לא נעשה בזה כלום. ובשביל אהבת אינשי בעלמא, נמי לא שייך לשמוח עולמית בשביל דבר שאירע לאינשי בכמה מאות שנים אחר כך. וזה נחשב מעשה אמורי - מה שחזינן שכמה דברים אירע לאינשי בכל יום עניני צער ואין מצטערין עליהן, וכמה עניני שמחה ואין שמחין עמהן, אף באותו הזמן ממש. ובעניין זה שמחין בעשיית וקביעת יום להילולא וחינגא ואכילת בשר תרנגול הודו אף כמה מאות שנים אח"כ, **שזה נחשב דבר שאין בו טעם, אלא הוא דרכי האמורי שעושין דברים בלא טעם ובלא צורך. ולכן איכא בזה האיסור דובחוקותיהם לא תלכו.**

This [prohibition of imitating Gentile customs] applies in instituting a day of festivity for this [historical] event, namely, that [these immigrants] when coming to this country for a time [after their arrival] had nothing to eat, and [thus] they ate turkey. [This event] was not significant for the settling of America, since America already had an ample supply of food for most of [the immigrants] who came even then. There were several species of fruit and other fowl, domesticated and wild animals, and fish in the lakes and rivers. Even if some people happened to be in a certain place at a time without fruits, and it was difficult to procure large cattle and wild game and [therefore] they ate turkey, even if those people had nothing to eat, since the world already knew about America, other people would have [certainly] arrived in ships with various foods and seeds to plant, and the country of America would have been settled [anyway] even without [those settlers eating turkey]. [Consequently], for the general populace [we find that] no [salvation] occurred. [Even for the purpose of showing] thanks for everyday individuals, [this] is [an] insufficient [reason to rejoice permanently [on this day]: [to celebrate a historical event] [in the name] of [gratitude for] something which happened to individuals hundreds of years later. This is considered "the ways of the *Emorites*" since the [Gentile populace] see many tragic events happening to people every day, and they do not commiserate with them. [They also know of] many joyous events and do not share that joy even at that time. But concerning this matter [only], they are joyous in the formation and institution of a day of festivity and the eating of turkey even hundreds of years later. **This is considered something without a [sufficient] reason and falls under the category of "the ways of the *Emorites*" who do things without reason or need. Therefore, [such celebration] is included in the prohibition of following Gentile customs.**

However, Rabbi Feinstein acknowledges that there is an understanding of the prohibition of "imitating Gentiles" where the reason for the practice does not have to be one that would be sufficient for Jews to establish a permanent celebration. Rather, if there is a valid reason for the practice and if it is not one established for religious reasons and is simply a commemoration, this would be permitted. In the case of Thanksgiving, he draws a significant distinction in the issue of idolatry between a practice that was established by idolatrous clergy versus a practice that was established by practitioners of a religion like the Pilgrims. Furthermore, while Rema only explicitly permits customs with well-known and understood reasons, perhaps he is not coming to exclude foolish reasoning from the prohibition. Additionally, he states that merely celebrating Thanksgiving does not contain a concern of prohibited addition of a holiday, because this is not established as a holiday by Jews but rather is a holiday of the Gentiles in the country where they live.

אבל אפשר לפרש שלעניין האיסור דלאו ובחוקותיהם לא תלכו, אין צורך בהיתרו לטעם שהיה מועיל גם לדינא לנו לעשות שמחה קבועה לזה אם היה אירע זה לישראל. אלא סגי להתיר בטעם שמועיל למנהגא דאינשי אף הנכרים, דכיוון שאין עושין זה בשביל עניני דתיהם, ולא בטעמי דתיהם, אלא הוא לזכר דבר שלא שייך לדתיהם, שלא נעשה זה ע"י כומרים אלא ע"י אינשי דעלמא שלא היו אדוקין בדתי ע"ז שלהן. כיוון שאין עושין זה מצד שייכות לדת שום ע"ז שבעולם, אין בזה משום ובחוקותיהם לא תלכו. ואף שבמה שמסיק הרמ"א שם בדוגמא להיתר מחמת שיש לדבר טעם במלבוש המיוחד לרופאים הוא טעם המובן ממש, וכן מה שעושין לכבוד, והיה מקום לומר שרק בכהאי גוונא ליתא לאיסור דובחוקותיהם, מ"מ נימא שלא בא הרמ"א למעט טעמים אחרים אף טעמים הפחותין מהם. ומצד זה שמדיני התורה אין יכולין לעשות שום קביעות חג מצד איזה מעשה, ואיכא גם משום בל תוסיף, הא אינו עושה ליום טוב בדיני ישראל אלא עושה זה מצד מנהג הנכרים אנשי המדינה. שא"כ ליכא איסור מצד בידוי מצווה ובל תוסיף, וגם לא משום הליכה בחוקות הגוים.

But it is possible to explain that regarding the [aforementioned prohibition], there is no need [for us to require a Gentile practice to have] a reason [for observance] that would [also] be effective *halachically* for us to create a fixed [day of] festivity [in remembrance] of a particular [event] if it would occur to the Jewish people. Rather, to permit [such a practice for Jews], a sensible reason for [creating] a custom for [Gentile] people, even [religious] Gentiles, would suffice. Since they are not observing [the custom] because of topics relating to their religion nor for [any] reasons relating to their religion, but rather for a [mundane] matter unrelated to their religion, [and since] it was not formed by [Christian] priests but rather through ordinary individuals who were not [necessarily] meticulous in their idolatrous religions, [and furthermore] since they are not founding [the holiday] because of its relevance to any idolatrous religion in the world, [observance of the holiday] does not violate following Gentile customs. Even though Rema concludes by giving a permissible example [of Gentile customs which he permits] because the custom has a reason, such as a uniform for doctors and [that] this reason is readily understood, and [the same would apply] [for] things done in honor [of the deceased], and [thus] there would be room to [argue] that only in such cases [where the reason is readily apparent] the [aforementioned] prohibition does not apply, nevertheless, one could suggest that Rema is not coming to exclude [activities with] other, even inferior, reasons [from this permit]. [Additionally,] from the perspective that from *Torah* law one cannot establish any fixed holiday for any event and [that] there is also [a violation] of [the prohibition of] adding to the *Torah*, [the celebrator of Thanksgiving] is not establishing a holiday in [*Torah* law] but is following the custom of the Gentiles, the citizens of the country [the United States]. Consequently, there is no prohibition of inventing a *mitzvah*, nor of adding to the Torah, nor of following Gentile practices.

Rabbi Feinstein notes that his interpretation of Rema,[15] which counts frivolous practices under the prohibition of Gentile customs, is not the only interpretation, and that one could also read Rema as only restricting an explicitly immoral practice. If one were to interpret Rema in the latter fashion, then the only prohibition of Thanksgiving would be that one cannot establish the Thanksgiving meal as an obligatory or annual practice, because this would be a prohibited *Torah* addition. However, Rabbi Feinstein personally prefers the former interpretation of Rema and in combination with his view that Thanksgiving does not carry a sufficient justification for existence, feels any celebration should be prohibited.

ורמזתי שיש לי עדיין ספק בזה בסוף תשובה ראשונה, וגם באיסור זה אינו ברור, ויש לעיין עוד. ולכן בתשובה שניה בעניין זה שהיה אחר זה, הזכרתי שעכ"פ איכא איסור לקבוע זה, וגם אף פעם אחת - לא לחובה ולמצווה אלא לשמחת הרשות, ולא בכל שנה. שלכן מאחר שלא היה לי ברור שאיכא הלאו, כתבתי בתשובה שניה שבהזדמנות אין לאסור כשאין כוונתו לחובה ולמצווה אלא לשמחת הרשות. וגם הא שייך לפרש דהרמ"א אינו אוסר אף בליכא טעם למנהג הגויים, אלא דווקא באיכא שייכות פריצות ולא בעשיית סעודה בעלמא. ואף אם אצל נכרים כל סעודה איכא בה גם פריצות, אבל הא ישראל רוצים לעשות סעודה כדרך סעודת ישראל שליכא בה פריצות. אבל אני בעצמי נוטה דעתי יותר דאיכא איסור הלאו דובחוקותיהם לא תלכו, אך לא מאיסורי ע"ז כדלעיל, שאין לחשוש בכגון דא לדרכי האמורי, אבל מכל מקום אסור משום שהוא חוק לגויים. שכן משמע יותר לשון הרמ"א בסופו בדברים המותרים שכתב אבל דבר שנהגו לתועלת וכו' או טעם אחר מותר, ששם יש יותר לדייק עניין המותר שהוא דווקא בדבר שיש בו תועלת ממש מבירישא שנקט עניין האיסור שכתב שאינו אסור אלא בדבר שנהגו בו משום פריצות וכו' או בדבר שנהגו למנהג ולחוק ואין טעם בדבר דאיכא ביה למיחש משום דרכי האמורי, והיה

---

[15] YD 178:1.

מקום לדייק שבדבר שאין לחשוש בו משום פריצות או דרכי האמורי מותר. ומכל מקום הדיוק מסוף הדברים, שגם מה שאין בו תועלת אף שאין לחשוש בו משום דרכי האמורי אסור. והוא כמו שכתבתי בתשובה הקודמת. אך כתבתי בתשובה שלאחריה שאף אם נימא דליכא הלאו, איכא עכ"פ איסור לעשות זה לחובה ולמצווה, אלא רק לשמחת הרשות ולא לקבוע זה בכל שנה.

At the end of the first responsum [O.C. 5:20:6], I alluded [to the fact] that I am still uncertain and this prohibition [of celebrating Thanksgiving] is not clear-cut and additional analysis is required. Consequently, in the second responsum about this matter [Y.D. 4:11:4], I mentioned that minimally it is prohibited to [permanently] establish this [holiday], and even observing it one time cannot be done from a sense of obligation or religious commandment but [only] as an optional celebration, and not every year. Since it was not entirely clear to me that the prohibition [of not following Gentile customs] applied, I wrote in the second responsum that one cannot prohibit occasional [celebration] when his intent is [only to do so] as an optional celebration, and not as an obligation or religious commandment. Additionally, one can interpret Rema as not prohibiting [Gentile practices] even if there is [an insufficient] reason for the Gentile custom unless immorality is involved, and not [for] the mere scheduling of a [festive] meal. Even if for the Gentiles, all festive meals include immorality, Jews [who] wish to celebrate in accordance with Jewish norms, which lack immorality, [may do so]. However, I myself lean more toward the perspective that the prohibition of following Gentile customs does apply. But [Thanksgiving is] not [forbidden] because of prohibitions forbidding idolatry as [explained] earlier, since there is no concern in matters such as this for "the ways of the *Emorites*." Nonetheless, it is prohibited because of [following] Gentile practices, since such is the more likely implication of Rema's language at the end of his words [concerning] permissible [practices], where he writes "but a matter that they practice for a benefit ... or some other reason, is permissible." [From this phraseology] it is more likely to infer that a permissible practice is something for which there is a real benefit [and not an insignificant reason]. [This is opposed to the implication of the phraseology at the] beginning [of Rema] where he writes concerning prohibited practices, "it is only prohibited in matters they practice because of immorality... or a matter practiced as a custom and statute without reason, where we need to be concerned of "the ways of the *Emorites*." [From this phraseology,] one can infer that a practice about which there is no concern of immorality or "the ways of the *Emorites*" is permissible. Nonetheless, the inference from his concluding words is that anything without a benefit even if there is no concern of "the ways of the *Emorites*" is prohibited. This is in accordance with what I wrote in the former responsum [to be strict, O.C. 5:20:6]. Nonetheless, in the latter responsum [*Y.D.* 4:11:4], I wrote that even if you were to say there is no negative commandment [of following Gentile practices which would be violated], there is still minimally a prohibition to arrange such [festivity] as an obligation and commandment. [It is only permitted] as an optional celebratory event and not to establish [the celebration] each year.

Rabbi Feinstein recognizes that there could be contradictory implications from his *teshuvot*. If one assumes that this is an issue of imitating Gentiles, according to his reading of Rema, then even having a single Thanksgiving dinner would be prohibited, although one would still be able to have a celebration on that day or a festive meal that is not intended to be for the Thanksgiving celebration.[16] However, if one assumes this is not an issue, according to the more lenient reading of Rema, then so long as one does not view it as obligatory, even if the meal is to commemorate the day, this would not be prohibited.[17] He concludes by stating that it is proper to be stringent like the first view but does not prohibit the meal.

ובעצם יש חילוק לדינא. דלתשובה הקודמת דאיכא הלאו דהליכה בחוקות הגוים, אסור אף פעם אחת בהזדמנות, אך אינו נאסר בשביל זה מלעשות איזה שמחה ביום זה, וגם סעודת מרעות בעלמא בלא כוונה לחשיבות היום. ולטעם תשובה אחרת ליכא איסור בהזדמנות שלא לכוונת חובה ומצווה אף שהוא בשביל כוונת חשיבות היום שעושין הנכרים, ומהראוי להחמיר כתשובה הקודמת.

ומש"כ הרמב"ן שעל הוספת חג איכא איסור בל תוסיף, ופי' מה שאיתא בירושלמי (מגילה פרק א' הלכה ה' דף ו' ע"ב בדפוס ווילנא) שמונים וחמשה זקנים ומהם שלשים וכמה נביאים היו מצטערים על הדבר הזה, אמרו כתיב אלה המצות אשר צוה ה' את משה, אילו המצוות שנצטווינו מפי משה, כך אמר לנו משה אין נביא אחר עתיד לחדש לכם דבר מעתה, ומרדכי ואסתר מבקשים לחדש לנו דבר, עד שהאיר הקדוש ברוך הוא את עיניהם וכו', הרי שהיתה המצווה הזאת אסורה להם, א"כ היא בכלל לא תוסיף, עיין שם. שא"כ יש לאסור לעשות יום שמחה קבוע לכל נס שיזדמן לישראל שיהיה כן בכל שנה ושנה מצד בל תוסיף. והימים טובים שנכתבו במגילת תענית, הוא רק

---

16 See first *teshuva* cited in this appendix, *EH* 2:13.

17 Although as Rabbi Feinstein stated earlier, one must be careful to always consider it voluntary and to not establish it as an annual occurrence.

לענין דלא לאיתענאה בהון ודלא למספד בהון שזה לא חשיבא הוספה. ולאמירת הלל בחנוכה נצטרך לומר דהוא מדאורייתא (כדביאר החתם סופר בדעת הרמב"ן בחלק או"ח סימן קס"א) ורק להדלקת נרות נצטרך לומר ששייך שיתקנו רבנן, והוא דוחק. ועיין במג"א סימן תרפ"ו סק"ה בשם הר"מ אלאשקר, שבני עיר שאירע להם נס באיזה יום יש להם לתקן בהסכמה ובחרם עליהם ועל הבאים אחריהם לעשות פורים באותו יום לעולם. ובסוף חיי אדם האריך בזה, וגם כתב שעשה מעשה בנס שנעשה לו ולבני ביתו, ולא הזכירו כלל מענין בל תוסיף. אך החי"א מחלק שם בין יחידים לציבור, ואולי גם המג"א סובר כן, אך שגם עיר כולה סובר דהוא כיחידים וצ"ע. עיין אג"מ ח"א דאו"ח סי' ט"ו ענף ג', בביאור שיטת הרמב"ן.

והנני זקנך אוהבך מאוד, משה פיינשטיין.

Essentially, there is a distinction [between the two responsa] in actual practice. According to the former responsum [O.C. 5:20:6] which [maintains that] the prohibition of following Gentile customs applies, it would be prohibited [to celebrate Thanksgiving Day] even one time in passing, but it would not be prohibited to schedule a [different] event [such as a *Bar Mitzvah* or wedding] on that day or a cordial meal not specifically in honor of the day. But according to the analysis of the other responsum [Y.D. 4:11:4], there would be no prohibition [to celebrate] occasionally without the intent for [it to become] an obligation or religious commandment, even if [such celebration] is in honor of the day celebrated by the Gentiles. It is appropriate to be stringent in accordance with the [conclusion of] the first responsum.

[Regarding] that which Ramban writes [in his commentary to Deuteronomy 4:2], that adding a[n obligatory] festival violates *bal tosif* [adding to the

Torah], and he explains [this passage] in the [Talmud] Yerushalmi (Megillah 1:5, 6b in the Vilna edition) "85 sages and among them thirty-something prophets were troubled by [Esther's adding on an obligatory holiday of Purim]. They stated, 'It is written, "These are the commandments which God commanded Moshe" [which means], these are the commandments we were commanded by Moshe. So said Moshe to us, "A later prophet will not add anything new," and Mordechai and Esther wish to do so!' Until Hashem enlightened their eyes ..." What emerges is that this commandment [of Purim] was prohibited for them, and, if so, it is included in the prohibition of adding to the Torah, see there [Megillah 1:5, 6b in the Vilna edition].[18] If so [that even Purim was challenged and became the sole exception], there is a prohibition forbidding the establishment of a set festive day every year [in honor of] any miracle occurring to Israel because of the prohibition of adding to the Torah. The festivals recorded in Megillat Ta'anit [a collection of minor festivals established mostly in the Second Temple era] are only [listing days where it is forbidden to] fast or deliver eulogies. [These practices] are not considered adding [to the Torah]. Concerning [adding] the recital of Hallel on Chanuka, we must say that it is of a Biblical nature (as explained by Chatam Sofer [Rabbi Moshe Sofer] O.C. 161 according to Ramban). Only concerning lighting candles, we must say that it is possible that the Rabbis can institute it, [even though] this is difficult. See Magen Avraham (O.C. 686:5) in the name of R. Moshe Al-Ashkar, that

---

[18] But according to the conclusion of that *Talmudic* passage, *Purim* was a specific exception.

> members of any town to which a miracle occurred can ordain with a collective decision, and [with the power to decree] excommunication [for those not accepting it] upon themselves and subsequent generations, to establish a *"Purim"*- [like holiday] on that day [of salvation] forever. At the end of *Chaye Adam* [155:41], [the author, R. Abraham Danzig writes] lengthily about this topic. He also writes that he himself acted on this ruling concerning a miracle which occurred to him and his family. The [above-mentioned scholars] did not mention the prohibition of adding to the Torah at all. However, the *Chaye Adam* distinguishes between an individual [who would be permitted] and the community, and perhaps Magen Avraham would agree [with him]. However, [*Chaye Adam* also] maintains that even an entire city is treated like [a group of] individuals [the prohibition only applies to a holiday established for the entire Jewish people]. This requires further study. See *Igrot Moshe O.C.* 1:15:3 [for an] explanation of the view of Ramban.
>
> I remain your grandfather who loves you very much,
>
> Moshe Feinstein

Rabbi Feinstein concludes by noting that celebrating Thanksgiving permanently does not necessarily violate *bal tosif* since prior rabbis discussed the ability of a community to declare permanent festive celebrations and meals in commemoration of a salvific event, so long as it stays local and is not obligatory for the entire Jewish people. Thus, Thanksgiving would be viewed as an acceptable American communal celebration without carrying the prohibition of adding to the *Torah*.

In summary, Rabbi Feinstein repeatedly defines Thanksgiving as a secular holiday that carries no concerns of idolatrous prohibitions, and thus scheduling unrelated celebrations on that day is completely permitted, although he notes that pious individuals should try to be stringent not to do so. Furthermore, the simple act of eating a turkey meal on Thanksgiving is also permitted.[19] However, on the topic of holding a Thanksgiving celebration or meal, Rabbi Feinstein seemingly presents two different answers. In one of his *teshuvot*,[20] he notes that holding a Thanksgiving meal is permitted, but only so long as it remains an optional event and does not become a permanent, obligatory meal every year. Thus, it emerges from this *teshuva*, that the only prohibition involved with Thanksgiving is establishing a command to hold a meal every year, which could violate the prohibition of *bal tosif*. However, in a different *teshuva*,[21] Rabbi Feinstein writes that even holding an optional Thanksgiving meal is prohibited. This is not due to a concern of idolatry, since Thanksgiving is secular, but rather due to a prohibition of imitating Gentile customs, which includes any secular custom with a senseless basis. Rabbi Feinstein argues that the holiday of Thanksgiving indeed serves no purpose: the historical event was not crucial in the settling of America since even if the Pilgrims had not succeeded, others would surely have taken their place. Meanwhile, assigning this one day alone as a celebration of gratitude and love for others in the present day is foolish.

To reconcile these two views, Rabbi Feinstein writes in a final *teshuva*[22] to his grandson, Rabbi Tendler, that the difference in his rulings is based on the interpretation of a key Rema which discusses the prohibition of imitating Gentile customs.[23] One could read Rema's opening clause as the normative *halacha*: that only immoral and baseless acts are included in this prohibition. According to this reading, the holiday of Thanksgiving would be permitted as an optional event just

---

[19] *Igrot Moshe YD* 4:11:4.

[20] Ibid.

[21] *Igrot Moshe OC* 5:20:6.

[22] *Igrot Moshe YD* 4:12.

[23] *YD* 178:1.

like Rabbi Feinstein wrote in his permissive *teshuva*. However, one could instead infer from Rema's concluding clause, which permits a practice containing a reasonable basis, that any foolish or insignificant basis for a practice is also prohibited. This accords with Rabbi Feinstein's stricter *teshuva* that prohibits any Thanksgiving celebrations, due to the basis for the holiday being insufficient in his eyes. Rabbi Feinstein writes that he personally prefers the stricter interpretation of Rema[24] which forbids any foolish practice, including Thanksgiving, but that such a view is not to be considered the normative *halacha*; rather, for ordinary individuals it is perfectly acceptable to celebrate Thanksgiving as an optional day of joy in America. Curiously, Rabbi Feinstein concludes this last *teshuva*, by noting that the issue of establishing a permanent meal for Thanksgiving might not be an issue, since prior authorities[25] allowed establishing such celebrations so long as they are only mandatory on that community and not on every Jew in the world.

---

[24] Rabbi Feinstein's preference to interpret Rema stringently could also be due to his mention in *Igrot Moshe* OC 5:20:6 of Tosfot who include all foolish practices in this prohibition.

[25] *Chaye Adam* 155:41.

Index:

American Independence Day, 47.

Antisemitism, 52.

Belsky, Rabbi Yisroel, 29, 32, 33, 34, 55.

Bleich, Rabbi J. David, 23, 39, 40, 41, 42, 94, 116, 117, 118.

Boston Thanksgiving Celebration, 13, 31.

Boudinot, Congressman Elias, 13.

Butler, Mr. Menachem, 9.

Chanukah, 18, 28, 43, 73, 126, 146.

Christmas, 18, 19, 25, 27, 45, 53, 54, 63, 72, 73, 75, 77, 98, 100, 122.

Cohen, Rabbi David, 23, 29, 36, 37, 41, 42, 45, 61, 89, 105, 107, 109, 110.

Cohen, Rabbi Feivel, 93-94.

Columbus Day, 12, 26, 27, 48, 53, 54.

Congregation Kehilath Jeshurun, 34.

Congregation Shearith Israel, 32, 33, 34.

Election Day, 26.

Ezrat Torah Calendar, 25, 27, 123.

Feinstein, Rabbi Moshe, 24-29, 35, 37, 40, 44, 45, 46, 47, 48, 49, 50, 52, 55, 68, 73, 76, 86, 99, 101, 114, 117, 121, 123, 125, 126, 128, 131, 134, 136, 138, 141, 144, 147, 148, 149.

Feldblum, Dr. Avi, 30, 31.

Fourth of July, 35, 100.

Good Friday, 18.

Gra (Rabbi Elijah of Vilna), 22, 23, 28, 35, 38, 98, 117.

Gregory the Great, St., 56, 65.

Greenblatt, Rabbi Ephraim, 28, 29, 40, 85-88, 113.

Hale, Sarah Josepha, 16.

Hallel, 28, 126, 146.

Halloween, 11, 53, 54, 55-64, 65, 66, 67.

Hammond, Governor James H., 15.

Henkin, Rabbi Yehuda Herzl, 34-36, 38, 40, 51, 55, 97-103.

Henkin, Rabbi Yosef Eliyahu, 27, 31, 49.

Hutner, Rabbi Yitzchak, 37-44, 45, 46, 50, 53, 89-92, 93, 94, 107, 108, 115.

Imitating Gentile customs, 20, 21, 22, 23, 24, 27, 30, 40, 68, 108, 118, 124, 136, 137, 148.

Jefferson, President Thomas, 15, 19.

King, Jr., Rev. Martin Luther, 48

Klein, Rabbi Menashe, 18, 29, 38, 40, 86, 99, 113-120.

Lamm, Rabbi Norman, 32, 33, 34,

Labor Day, 26, 46, 47, 48, 77.

Lincoln, President Abraham, 16, 17, 48,

Macy's Thanksgiving Day Parade, 45.

Miller, Rabbi Avigdor, 43.

Memorial Day, 26, 48, 77.

National Thanksgiving Holiday, 16.

National Thanksgiving Proclamation, 13, 33.

New Year's Day, 24-25, 27, 53, 54, 64, 71, 72, 73, 74, 75, 77, 122, 123.

October 1578 (Canadian Thanksgiving), 12.

October 1621 (First Thanksgiving Celebration), 13, 37.

Orthodox Union, 39.

Pilgrims, 12, 13, 38, 39, 41, 81, 117-118, 136, 139, 148.

Purim, 43, 60, 146, 147,

Puritans, 39, 40, 41, 117-118.

Reiss, Rabbi Yona, 43.

Schachter, Rabbi Hershel, 30, 86.

Shapiro, Dr. Marc, 31.

Soloveitchik, Rabbi Joseph B., 29, 30-36, 37, 44, 52, 53, 55, 86.

Turkey, 11, 20, 25, 26, 28, 29, 30, 31, 37, 38, 40, 41, 42, 43, 44, 55, 79, 80, 81, 82, 83, 86, 98, 107, 108, 113, 117, 118, 124, 125, 126, 129, 130, 133, 136, 137, 138, 148.

United States Constitution, 13, 14, 15.

Valentine's Day, 11, 53, 54, 65-69, 73.

Veterans Day, 26, 48, 53, 54.

Washington, President George, 13, 14, 16, 17, 19, 33, 48.

Weinberg, Rabbi Yechiel Yaakov, 20, 22, 23.

Yeshiva University, 30, 32, 34.

Yom Ha'atzma'ut, 46, 47.

Yom Hashoa, 46.

Yom Yerushalayim, 46.

Yosef, Rabbi Ovadiah, 37, 47, 83.

About the Author

Michael J. Broyde is a Professor of Law at Emory University, the director of its SJD program, and a Professor of Jewish Law at the Tam Institute of Jewish Studies at Emory. He is also the Berman Projects Director at the Emory University Center for the Study of Law and Religion. In the past, he has been the director of the Beth Din of America and one of its dayanim, the rabbi of the Young Israel in Atlanta, and the Rosh Kollel of a Torah MiTzion Kollel, as well as a visiting professor at Stanford Law School and many other schools, and a Senior Fulbright Scholar in Israel. This book is an expansion of an article published in 1995 in the Journal of Halacha and Contemporary Society. His works can be found at https://michaelbroyde.com.

Made in the USA
Columbia, SC
02 December 2024